Cut Flowers

A practical guide to their selection and care

3rd Edition

Su Whale NDSF FBFA

Photography by Mark Follon

Additional photography by Holly Peck

Oxypetalum caeruleum

Published by:

Jago Publishing Ltd.
23 Tomlan Road
West Heath
Birmingham
B31 3NX

info@jagopublishing.co.uk
www.jagopublishing.co.uk

First Published 2011
Second Edition 2014
Third Edition 2017

A CIP catalogue record for this book
is available from the British Library.

ISBN 978-0-9568713-3-6

Designed by Corner House Design and Print Ltd. Manchester
Printed in England by Coloprint Ltd. Birmingham

Contents

Fritillaria persica 'Ivory Bells'

Introduction

 People from a planet without flowers would think we must be mad with joy the whole time to have such things about us

Iris Murdoch

Welcome to 'Cut Flowers' third edition! Thoroughly revised, it contains three new flowers so there are now 156 of the most popular cut flowers featured in total. Despite its third make-over, the essence of the book remains the same, a practical guide on flower care aimed at florists, floristry students, flower arrangers and indeed anyone who just loves to have flowers in the home.

For those of you picking up this book for the first time, this is not a botanical or gardening encyclopaedia, but a floral reference book – in here you will find flower availability, colour range, care tips, advice on display, uses in wedding work and some incidental trivia. Every flower has been photographed in full colour and pages are arranged in alphabetical order of botanical names (there is also an index of common names for easy cross reference). Plus a new page has been added with tips on what to look for when choosing and buying cut flowers.

What was really fantastic about publishing the first edition back in 2011 was the reception, not just from the floristry industry, but from flower lovers who were not professionally involved in floristry but who enjoyed having flowers in their home. Having worked as a florist for over twenty years I'm very proud that with these books I am helping to contribute to the movement of encouraging people to visit their local florist to buy their flowers, and I hope this revised and expanded edition will continue the work of the previous two.

In 2013 after two years of research, I published the companion book 'Cut Foliage A practical guide to its selection and care' with the same aims of the flower book, to be useful and practical, for after all, what is a vase of flowers or an arrangement without foliage to support and complement it? This was also fully revised before it was reprinted in 2015.

Both books have been well received so I would also like to take this opportunity to once again give a big 'thank you' to everyone who, over the last six years have bought the books and been so positive about them, from college students, to lecturers, to florists and flower arrangers – your support has been and still is much appreciated!

Enjoy your flowers!

'Cut Flowers A practical guide to their selection and care'

This book has been a labour of love for Su Whale. Several years ago she approached me and told me of her idea of writing a book that would facilitate flower identification. As the years progressed, the original concept developed into something much more and the reality is that Su has created a handbook that should be an essential piece of equipment for every floral art/floristry/gardening student in the world not to mention florists, flower arrangers, brides and hobbyists too. This little book covers more than 150 flower varieties in normal use for arranging and tells you about availability, vase life, tips on arranging in the home and suitability for weddings etc. We have watched in admiration as Su tackled this very necessary subject matter and have been privileged to watch the project's development. The photography by Mark Follon is quite superb!

Alison Bradley, Fusion Flowers Magazine – www.fusionflowers.com

Based on her experience in the world of flowers, Su Whale decided to publish a book with detailed information on over 150 varieties of cut flowers. The correct name of the flower, the availability, the vase life, which colours. In addition, it offers specific information for florists, floristry students attending training, and also for home care. Everyone who loves cut flowers will find some valuable information in this convenient book.

Fleur Creatif Magazine

'Cut Flowers' by Su Whale really is **the** reference book for florists, students and everyone who loves flowers. With succinct fact files on well-known blooms, it's the perfect way to familiarise yourself with the wonderful world of all things floral!

Rona Wheeldon, Founder of Flowerona, Writer & Trainer

Reviews of 'Cut Foliage A practical guide to its selection and care'

After the success of Cut Flowers, there is now Cut Foliage. This book gives practical advice about the use of greenery in floral arrangements. You will find more than 140 types of green, both commercially grown and from the garden. The clear instructions are complemented with information about availability and durability. You will also find information on suitability and use in all sorts of floral creations. An indispensable guide for cutting green materials.

Fleur Creatif Magazine

How to use this book

A page has been devoted to each flower, laid out in the same order for ease of reference.

Botanical Name: The flowers are arranged in alphabetical order of botanical names.

Common Name: These are some of the common names by which the flower is otherwise known.

Availability: Based on information from the Dutch flower auctions. As The Netherlands are the world's biggest exporter of cut flowers this is most likely where your florist or wholesaler will be sourcing them from. Due to advances in production, many previously seasonal flowers are now available all year round, although it is important to bear in mind that weather, as well as local/national events can, and indeed do, affect supply.

Vase Life: The typical life of the flower if conditioned correctly and kept in optimum conditions either in the flower shop or at home. Buying flowers out of season can result in a shorter vase life.

Flower Notes: Some general background information to give a 'feel' to the flower. This includes stem length. Wary that eyes can glaze over when numbers are involved, short, medium and tall are used instead. As actual measurements, they are as follows:

Short stem length: 10cm–30cm (4"–12") e.g. Muscari up to tulip.

Medium stem length: 30cm–55cm (12"–22") e.g. tulip up to standard carnation.

Tall stem length: 55cm–90cm (22"–36") e.g. standard carnation up to Strelitzia and above.

Colour Range: Based on the colour range available as a commercial cut flower, which doesn't necessarily reflect the full colour range of the flower as found growing in the garden.

For the Florist: Advice on conditioning, storing and displaying in a commercial environment. This covers:

Temperature Range: For storage and ideally for display if possible.

Stem type: Included where it is felt that knowledge of the stem type would be helpful with conditioning. For further information on stem types, please refer to the glossary.

Flower Form: I have based these on the most simple of definitions, intended to assist as a guide in the selection of flowers for a design. See the glossary for explanation of terms.

(I haven't in this section mentioned re-cutting stems on arrival – I am assuming that this is done automatically by the florist!)

For the Home: Advice on looking after the flower at home plus some suggestions on display and flowers to complement it. Also instructions on how to dry if appropriate.

How to use this book

For Weddings:
Comments on the flower's suitability for weddings including bridal, reception and venue designs, plus whether or not the flower can be used in wired work. This is to help brides, florists and flower arrangers in their choice of flowers and is based on over 20 years in commercial floristry so by definition is slightly subjective – feel free to experiment! This also includes the flower meaning should there be one.

For Students:
Family and Genus: Flower groups are frequently being reclassified as more is discovered about their botanical make-up. Where there has been conflicting information, I have used the Royal Horticultural Society (RHS) as a benchmark.
Origin: Where the flower first originated, not necessarily where it has now naturalised.
Flower Trivia: Amazing what you didn't know!

Symbols:

 Seasonally grown in the UK This flower is grown in the British Isles. These tend to be seasonally available rather than all year round. Bear in mind that our unpredictable weather can have a big effect on the availability of home grown flowers.

 Can be dried This flower can be preserved at home by drying.

 Fragrant A flower with a highly developed fragrant scent.

 Pungent flower A flower with a strong scent which is not necessarily fragrant, such as Allium.

 Irritant 'Ouch!' This is a flower where either the sap or the flower itself can have an irritant quality, such as producing a skin rash or where it may be prickly to the touch.

 Poisonous Unless you definitely know a flower is edible, it's generally not a good idea to eat it. However some flowers, such as Aconitum are extremely poisonous and should be handled accordingly.

 Specialist flower food available It is possible to obtain flower food which has been developed for flowers that have more specific requirements, such as shrubs, roses and flowers grown from bulbs. Ordinary flower food can be substituted if the specialised food isn't available.

And finally…the flower symbol. This is to indicate the size of the flower in real life compared to the photograph in the book.

Many of the flowers are actual size which is indicated thus:

Half size of photograph

One and a half times size of photograph

Twice size of photograph

And so on!

Choosing fresh flowers for the home

Where to buy
Your local flower shop
If you are lucky enough to have a florist shop or flower stall in your vicinity, then this is the place to head to. An experienced and trained florist will be able to give you plenty of advice and help you with your selection, and you will also have the luxury of being able to buy single stems as well as bunches of flowers.

Supermarkets
It would be unfair of me not to say that it is perfectly possible to buy quality flowers from some supermarkets and high street retailers, what they are lacking however is the knowledge and care that you would get from a professional florist. In my experience, once the flowers have been unpacked and displayed in a supermarket, scant attention is often paid to them afterwards!

Buying by the bunch
If buying flowers pre-bunched, check the colour and condition of the foliage, as they tend to sweat in the cellophane, if it is yellow or slimy then the flowers are old. If buying from a supermarket, check the water level in the bucket as flowers left in little or sometimes no water at all is a common problem with supermarket flowers. Also check for any damaged heads and prominent pollen stamens – this means that the flowers are mature.

Buying by the stem
When choosing individual flowers, look for strong stems and green healthy foliage, there should be no foliage below the water line of the vase and the water should be clean and fresh.

Carnations – the white stamens should not be showing in the centre, check for brown edges to the calyx underneath and the flower itself it should feel bouncy, not flaccid.

Chrysanthemums – if the centre is visible it should be green and solid to the touch with no pollen evident.

Gerberas – look for unmarked and pert petals, if they have a slight bluish tinge, they have been kept too long in cold storage.

Lilies – buy in bud for maximum vase life at home. If closed buds are flaccid to the touch and brown at the tips then they will probably not open. The foliage should be a fresh green, not yellow.

Roses – a gentle squeeze at the base of the flower head will tell if the rose if fresh or not, it should be firm, not soft. However some garden style roses now available commercially already arrive in a semi-open state. Your florist will be able to advise!

Tropical Flowers
Brown markings and a sticky appearance indicate that the flower is mature – this applies especially to Strelitzia and Heliconia. Anthuriums, like Gerberas, turn a bluish shade when they have been exposed to low temperatures.

A few do's and don'ts

When it comes down to basic requirements, flowers are like us– they need clean water, fresh air and food to stay healthy. Keep this in mind and there is no reason why you shouldn't enjoy your flowers for their maximum vase life.

Good housekeeping
Always place flowers in a clean vase or container, as bacteria inside grubby vases will pollute the water and shorten your flower's life.

What kind of water?
Ordinary tap water is fine. There are no particular benefits to using lukewarm water, although ice cold water can help to dissolve any air bubbles that might be in the stem.

How much water in the vase?
Obviously this depends on the size of the vase, but unless your flowers need to stand in shallow water (e.g. Gerberas) then approximately two-thirds is about right. If you have an opaque vase, don't forget to top it up.

Re-cutting stems
This is important! When flowers are out of water their stem ends will seal over, so you must always re-cut stems before placing your flowers in water, taking off about 2cm (1"). Once in the vase, stems can also become blocked with bacteria which reduce their ability to take up water. Re-cutting the stems of your flowers every few days will make a huge difference to their vase life.

Re-cut stems at an angle of approximately 45° (unless they are hollow in which case they should be left flat) this exposes a larger area to absorb water and means the stem ends aren't sitting flat on the base of the container

And please don't bash or split woody stems – it just mashes up vital capillaries which are responsible for taking water up to the flower head. Not good for the flowers at all.

Flower Food – to add or not to add...
All flowers need clean water and most of them need feeding as well. Commercial flower food has been developed to meet both of those needs; it will keep bacteria at bay and provide necessary nutrients to the flower. 'Home grown' remedies such as using bleach, copper pennies or aspirin do part of that job, but not all of it. (Bleach should be avoided as it burns the stems and leaves).

Foliage
Remove all foliage that will be in contact with water as over time it will decay and pollute the water, shortening your flower's vase life.

Displaying flowers at home
Flowers don't enjoy being in direct heat, so display them away from fires, radiators and out of direct sunlight – a cool spot with good air circulation is ideal.

Roses – dealing with 'bent neck'
In most cases this problem occurs in roses that have been harvested too early so their stems are too weak to support the flower heads. Prolonged dry storage leading to dehydration can also cause this condition. Try re-cutting the stems and submerging the entire flower in water for a short period before placing in a clean vase with specialised rose flower food.

Acacia

Common Name: **Golden Acacia, Mimosa, Wattle, Thorntree**

Availability: December–April, peaks February–March.

Vase Life: 5–7 days.

Flower Notes: Pronounced 'A-KAY-c-a'. A woody stemmed shrub with brightly coloured racemes of flowers that have a soft, woolly appearance and delicate, fern-like leaves. Medium stem length.

Colour Range: Bright yellow.

For the Florist:

- Ideal temperature range: 2–5°C (36–41°F).
- Re-cut stems and leave in plastic wrapping, although be careful that it doesn't sweat.
- Stand in fresh, clean water and condition thoroughly before use.
- Store away from direct heat and draughts and don't overcrowd containers.
- Extremely sensitive to ethylene gas.

For the Home:

- To get the best out of mimosa, use in vase designs and keep containers topped up.
- Remove all foliage in contact with water and display out of direct sunlight.
- Change water every 2 -3 days, using flower food to encourage development.
- Stems have small thorns, handle with care.
- Arrange with other seasonal spring flowers such as Narcissus and tulips.

For Weddings:

Tactile and attractive, mimosa would be a welcome addition to spring bridal designs, although some brides might be put off by its bright yellow hue! It's perfect however for contrasting with lime, crisp white and orange although its use is limited in more subtle colour schemes. Unsuitable for wiring.

Flower Meaning: Friendship.

 Acacia dealbata

For Students:

Family: Mimosaceae.

Genus: Acacia.

Origin: Majority of species from Australia.

Flower Trivia: Bunches of mimosa are traditionally handed out to women in Italy on International Woman's Day.

Achillea

Availability: March–November, peaks April–October.

Vase Life: Approx 7–14 days.

Flower Notes: Pronounced 'A-KILL-e-a'. Flowers form a flat, broad-headed cluster on a slim stem. Very common as a wild flower and popular in dried arrangements. It has a distinctive 'peppery' smell. Medium stem length.

Colour Range: Yellow, gold, terracotta, pink, peach, white.

For the Florist:

- Ideal temperature range 2–4°C (36–39°F).
- Avoid overcrowding vases as this can rot the stems and turn the flower heads mouldy.
- Change water every 2–3 days.
- **Form:** Round.

For the Home:

- Re-cut stems and remove all foliage in contact with water.
- Change water every other day.
- Arrange with flowers in autumnal shades such as Amaranthus, Physalis and Dahlia.
- If drying Achillea, remove all foliage from the stems and hang upside down in small bunches in a dark, cool place with good air circulation. They should take between 3–4 weeks to dry and can be used for up to a year.

 Achillea filipendulina 'Moonshine'

For Weddings:

A natural wild flower, lovely for a traditional country style wedding, suitable for tied posies and arrangements.
The gold colours of 'Moonshine' and 'Parkers Variety' would be particularly effective in autumnal wedding designs.
Flower Meaning: A cure for heartaches.

For Students:

Family: Asteraceae.
Genus: Achillea.
Origin: Europe and Asia.
Flower Trivia: Attractive to butterflies, the leaves of Achillea are also said to relieve toothache.

Aconitum

Common Name: **Monkshood, Wolfsbane, Devil's helmet**

Availability: January–November.

Vase Life: Approx 10–12 days.

Flower Notes: Pronounced 'Ack-O-nigh-tum'. Slim and sturdy, Aconitum has intensely coloured hooded flowers with black centres. A popular garden flower, it can also be found growing in the wild. Extremely poisonous. Tall stem length.

Colour Range: Deep purple, dark blue, pale blue.

For the Florist:

- Ideal temperature range 7–10°C (44–50°F).
- Lower temperatures can cause the flowers to turn black.
- Remove all foliage in contact with water.
- Always wash hands and clean workbench after use.
- **Form:** Line.

For the Home:

- Re-cut stems and place in clean, fresh water.
- Remove any leaves in contact with water.
- Change water every 2–3 days and add flower food.
- Due to its poisonous qualities, not recommended in households with small children or inquisitive pets.
- Wear gloves when handling if possible and always wash hands after use.
- Arrange with large-headed flowers such as roses and lilies.

 Aconitum napellus

For Weddings:

This flower would be great for a gothic wedding, as its rich purple colour would mix perfectly with deep reds and black. Suitable for large pedestal designs or simply massed together in tall vases. Not recommended in tied posies or for wiring work. **Flower Meaning:** Beware! Danger is near.

For Students:

Family: Ranunculaceae.

Genus: Aconitum.

Origin: Western and Central Europe.

Flower Trivia: Credited with supernatural powers, Aconitum was believed to turn people into werewolves should they eat any part of it.

Agapanthus

Common Name: **African lily, Lily of the Nile**

Availability: January to December, with different varieties peaking within that period.

Vase Life: Approx 4–6 days as the flower opens, then a further 7–14 in flower.

Flower Notes: Pronounced 'AG-a-pan-thus'. A hugely popular garden flower and a favourite of landscape designers due to its large showy spherical head and upright, leafless stem. Tall stem length.

Colour Range: Blue, purple, white.

For the Florist:

- Ideal temperature range 1–5°C (34–41°F).
- Prone to flower drop, to help prevent this, re-cut stems frequently to keep a fresh flow of water to the flower head.
- Never leave out of water as the flower dries out easily.
- Benefits from the use of flower food.
- **Form:** Round.

For the Home:

- Re-cut stems and stand in clean, fresh water with flower food.
- Change water every 2–3 days, re-cutting stems each time.
- Agapanthus has a strong sturdy stem and is equally effective arranged in a vase or in floral foam – if using foam, ensure it is soaked thoroughly before use and is not allowed to dry out.
- Arrange with tall, bold flowers such as gladioli or lilies.

 Agapanthus 'Blue Horizon'

For Weddings:
Smaller headed Agapanthus are suitable for using in both bridal bouquets and tied posies. Dramatic and eye-catching, larger headed varieties would stand out in arrangements either in vases or in floral foam. Perfect summer wedding flowers!

For Students:
Family: Agapanthaceae.
Genus: Agapanthus.
Origin: South Africa.
Flower Trivia: Its name comes from ancient Greek and means 'love flower'.

Ageratum

Common Name: **Floss flower, Blue mink**

Availability: All year round, scarce in December.

Vase Life: Approx 7–10 days.

Flower Notes: Pronounced 'A-JER-rah-tum'. Miniature clumps of fluffy, brush-like flower heads on soft stems with bright green foliage, often grown as a bedding plant. Medium stem length.

Colour Range: Pale lilac blue, white.

For the Florist:

- Ideal temperature range 1–2°C (34–36°F).
- If delivered 'dry', re-cut stems and put into water straight away, as Ageratum wilt quickly.
- Remove all foliage in contact with water.
- **Form:** Transitional.

For the Home:

- Re-cut stems and place in clean, fresh water with flower food.
- Ageratum will last longer arranged in water than in floral foam.
- Remove all foliage below the water line.
- Keep out of direct sunlight and draughts.
- Add to bolder summer flowers such as scabious and larkspur.

Ageratum houstonianum
'Blue Horizon'

For Weddings:

On its own Ageratum is a rather insignificant flower, but its delicate shades of lilac-blue make it a useful addition in tied posies for a spring or summer wedding. Stems are a little too soft for wired work.

For Students:

Family: Asteraceae.
Genus: Ageratum.
Origin: Mexico and Peru.
Flower Trivia: The name comes from the ancient Greek meaning 'that which does not age'.

Ajania

Common Name: **Pacific Chrysanthemum**

Availability: All year round.

Vase Life: Approx 10–21 days.

Flower Notes: Pronounced 'A-JANE-e-a'. A somewhat overlooked pretty perennial with button-like flowers and attractive silvery foliage. Extremely long lasting. Medium stem length.

Colour Range: Mustard yellow.

For the Florist:

- Ideal temperature range 2–5°C (34–41°F).
- Remove all foliage in contact with water.
- Change water every 4–5 days, re-cutting stems each time.
- **Form:** Transitional.

For the Home:

- Re-cut stems and place in clean, fresh water with flower food.
- Very long lasting, change water weekly, re-cutting stems every time.
- Use Ajania to show off larger headed flowers such as sunflowers and carnations.

Ajania pacifica Yellowday

For Weddings:

Not an obvious flower to pick for a wedding, although Ajania would be a dependable filler flower for reception and church arrangements and would coordinate happily with an autumnal colour theme.

For Students:

Family: Asteraceae.

Genus: Chrysanthemum.

Origin: Central and Eastern Asia.

Flower Trivia: Very popular with gardeners as a decorative foliage plant and for providing late autumn colour in the garden.

Alchemilla

Common Name: **Lady's mantle**

Availability: April–November, peaks May–September.

Vase Life: Approx 7–10 days.

Flower Notes: Pronounced 'Al-ka-milla'. Small frothy clouds of tiny flowers rise above large soft leaves covered in silky hairs. A typical cottage garden flower, also found growing in the wild. Medium stem length.

Colour Range: Lime green.

For the Florist:

- Ideal temperature range 1–2°C (34–36°F).
- Remove all foliage in contact with water which should be changed every 2–3 days, re-cutting stems each time.
- Keep out of strong sunlight and direct heat sources as these will dry out the flower.
- Mist occasionally.
- **Form:** Transitional.

For the Home:

- Re-cut stems and remove all foliage in contact with water.
- Change water every other day, flower food is recommended.
- Can be dried by hanging upside down in small bunches in a cool area with good air circulation.
- A pretty filler flower for vases, especially with large-headed summer flowers.

For Weddings:

Also classed as a wild flower, Alchemilla is perfect for a natural, country style wedding. Its limey colour will act as a foil to brighter, more vibrant tones. Lovely in natural tied posies and also lasts reasonably well in floral foam. Stems a little too soft for wired work.

For Students:

Family: Rosaceae.

Genus: Alchemilla.

Origin: Mediterranean.

Flower Trivia: The name comes from Arabic and means 'little magical one', due to its healing properties and the fact that its leaves catch the early morning dew.

Alchemilla mollis 'Robustica'

Allium

Common Name: **Ornamental onion**

Availability: March–September.

Vase Life: Approx 12–20 days.

Flower Notes: A firm favourite with landscape gardeners due to its distinctive spherical head of flowers which range in size from that of a golf ball up to the huge *Allium giganteum* which is over 20cm (8") in diameter. Tall stem length.

Colour Range: Purple, lavender, white.

For the Florist:

- Ideal temperature range 6–10°C (43–50°F).
- Always use fresh water and a clean vase to prevent contamination from slime which can form on the stems.
- Sensitive to bacteria, so always use flower food.
- Change water every other day, cleaning vase and rinsing stems at the same time.
- Form: Round.

For the Home:

- Re-cut stems and place in clean, fresh water.
- Change water every 2–3 days, flower food is recommended.
- Alliums form attractive green seed heads when mature.
- The scent of onion can sometimes be overpowering, but will not affect other flowers.

Allium sphaerocephalon

Allium 'Gladiator'

For Weddings:

The sculptural flowers of Allium would suit a contemporary wedding theme and would look impressive in large arrangements although in confined spaces some guests might find the scent of onion a little off-putting.

For Students:

Family: Alliaceae.

Genus: Allium.

Origin: Central Asia.

Flower Trivia: Allium is a member of the onion family, which, with over 1250 species, is one of the largest plant genera in the world.

17

Alpinia

Common Name: **Red ginger, Pink cone ginger, Ostrich plume**

Availability: September–May.

Vase Life: Approx 14–21 days.

Flower Notes: A showy, tropical flower with a satiny, almost prawn-like appearance. Can be grown as a specimen plant in a hothouse or conservatory. Tall stem length.

Colour Range: Lipstick pink, red.

For the Florist:

- Minimum storage temperature 13°C (55°F).
- Lower temperatures will cause the flower to blacken.
- Re-cut stems every 4–5 days, changing water each time.
- Soaking the heads in warm water will revive wilting flowers.
- Form: Line.

For the Home:

- Re-cut stems and place in clean, fresh water.
- Change water every 4–5 days, re-cutting stems each time.
- Avoid flowers with black or brown marks.
- Spraying occasionally will help to prolong vase life.
- Suitable for using in floral foam.
- The leaves of Alpinia can also be used in flower arrangements.

 Alpinia purpurata

For Weddings:
Unless a bride has chosen a tropical theme, these are not obvious candidates for weddings, although the shell-like, delicate pink of Alpinia would not look out of place in a summer ceremony when arranged with, for example, creamy white Anthuriums and Curcumas.

For Students:
Family: Zingiberaceae.
Genus: Alpinia.
Origin: Malaysia.
Flower Trivia: Alpinia is the national flower of Samoa, where it is commonly known as 'Teulia'.

Alstroemeria

Common Name: **Peruvian lily, Ulster Mary, Inca lily**

Availability: All year round.

Vase Life: Approx 7–14 days.

Flower Notes: Pronounced 'Al-STROE-meer-ria'. Trumpet-like with distinctive markings, Alstroemeria is reliable and popular; it is often packaged with netting around the heads to protect the flowers. Can cause an allergic reaction. Tall stem length.

Colour Range: All colours with the exception of blue and green.

For the Florist:

- Ideal temperature range 3–10°C (38–50°F). Sensitive to ethylene gas.
- The leaves damage easily, handle with care and do not stack flowers.
- Remove all foliage in contact with water, and change water every 3–4 days.
- Cut away any white parts of the stem.
- For best results, use specialised flower food.
- **Form:** Transitional.

For the Home:

- Re-cut stems and place in clean, fresh water.
- Use flower food, and change water every 3–4 days, re-cutting stems each time.
- Remove the majority of leaves from the stem to encourage water to go to the flower heads.
- They will last longer in cool conditions, so keep out of direct heat and sunlight.

 Alstroemeria 'Allure'

For Weddings:

As some people are allergic to Alstroemeria, it may be best to avoid using it in hand-tied posies. It lasts well in floral foam and is an ideal flower for filling out large pedestal arrangements. In summer, when the flowers are at their strongest they can be used in wired work.

For Students:

Family: Alstroemeriaceae.

Genus: Alstroemeria.

Origin: South America.

Flower Trivia: An odd characteristic of Alstroemeria is that the leaves on its stem grow upside down; there seems to be no definitive explanation as to why.

Amaranthus

Common Name: **Tassel flower, Love-lies-bleeding, Prince's feather**

Availability: April–December, peaks July–October.

Vase Life: Approx 8–12 days.

Flower Notes: Amaranthus has two distinctive styles, one a delicate, catkin-like trail with a dense, woolly texture, the other an upright spike, which despite its feathery look, is slightly prickly to the touch. Medium and tall stem length.

Colour Range: Crimson, red, russet, sage green, creamy green.

For the Florist:

- Ideal temperature range 8–10°C (46–50°F).
- A fragile flower, handle with care. Flower food is recommended.
- If flowers arrive 'dry', re-cut stems, wrap in paper and stand in fresh, cold water to revive them.
- Change water every other day.
- **Form: Line.**

For the Home:

- Re-cut stems at an angle and place in clean, fresh water with flower food.
- Amaranthus can give off a fine pollen when flowers are mature.
- Display out of direct sunlight, and change water every other day.
- To dry, remove all the leaves and hang upside down in a dry, warm spot with good ventilation.
- Arrange with large-headed textural flowers such as *Celosia cristata* or Dahlias.

Amaranthus cruentus 'Hot Biscuits'
Syn. *A. Paniculatus*

 Amaranthus cruentus 'Oeschberg'

For Weddings:
The texture and colours of Amaranthus are perfect for a winter/Christmas wedding. Add into tied posies with ivy, seasonal berries and red roses. The long, flexible fronds of the trailing varieties are extremely versatile in arrangements.
Flower Meaning: Not heartless.

For Students:
Family: Amaranthaceae.
Genus: Amaranthus.
Origin: South America.
Flower Trivia: Its botanical name comes from the Greek 'amarantos' meaning, 'one that does not wither'.

Ammi

Availability: All year round.

Vase Life: Approx 10–14 days.

Flower Notes: Similar in style to the hedgerow flower cow parsley, Ammi has delicate, pretty flowers on willowy stems with fern-like leaves. Tall stem length.

Colour Range: Creamy white.

For the Florist:

- Ideal temperature range 2–5°C (36–41°F).
- Change water every 3–4 days, re-cutting stems each time to ensure a flow of water to the flower head.
- Very similar is *Ammi visnaga* which has a more solid, less frothy appearance.
- **Form:** Round.

For the Home:

- Re-cut stems and place in clean, fresh water with flower food.
- Remove lower leaves to prevent water contamination and change water every 3–4 days, re-cutting stems each time.
- Keep out of direct heat and sunlight. It will shed fine white pollen as it matures.
- Arrange in a tall container with bold, large-headed flowers such as lilies, roses and peonies.

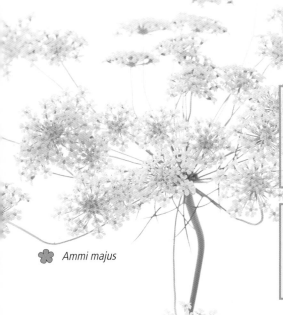

Ammi majus

For Weddings:
Ammi's wild hedgerow look makes it perfect for a very natural, vintage-style wedding. Although available all year round its light airy appearance would be lovely for a summer wedding. Ideal for bridal hand-tied bouquets and vase designs.

For Students:
Family: Apiaceae.
Genus: Ammi.
Origin: Mediterranean, North Africa.
Flower Trivia: Related to the wild carrot (*Daucus carota*).

Anemone

Common Name: **Garden Anemone, Poppy Anemone**

Availability: September–May, peaks December–April.

Vase Life: Approx 5–7 days, depending on room temperature.

Flower Notes: Pronounced 'A-NEN-oh-me'. A popular spring flower, richly coloured yet with a simple, open style of delicate cup-shaped papery petals and a dark velvety centre. Short stem length.

Colour Range: White, red, pale pink, cerise pink, mauve, purple, deep blue.

For the Florist:

- Optimum temperature 2°C (36°F).
- Allow time for the flowers to absorb water when first being conditioned.
- Anemones are thirsty flowers, so top up containers regularly.
- Benefits from using specialised bulb flower food.
- Can be re-hydrated by soaking the flower head in water for a short time.
- **Stem Type:** Hollow/Hairy.
- **Form:** Round.

Anemone coronaria

For the Home:

- Re-cut stems and place in clean, shallow water with flower food.
- Anemones will continue to grow in the vase and will curve naturally towards the light.
- They open rapidly in warm conditions, so stand in a cool, but light, spot.
- Arrange with similar sized spring flowers such as tulips and Ranunculus.

For Weddings:

A gorgeous flower for a spring wedding, but due to its delicate make-up should be handled with care. Can be used in floral foam if wired first, but looks its best when used in natural tied posies. Can be wired for buttonholes and corsages, but need gentle handling!

Flower Meaning: Sincerity.

For Students:

Family: Ranunculaceae.

Genus: Anemone.

Origin: Mediterranean and parts of Asia.

Flower Trivia: Anemone is a member of the buttercup family and has been used since Roman times for medicinal purposes, including the treatment of bruises and freckles.

Anethum

Common Name: **Dill**

Availability:	June–November.
Vase Life:	Approx 7–10 days.
Flower Notes:	Pronounced 'A-knee-thumb'. A flat, umbrella-shaped flower head consisting of tiny star-shaped flowers, it has a natural, hedgerow appearance. Tall stem length.
Colour Range:	Mustard yellow, pale yellow.

For the Florist:

- Ideal temperature range 2–5°C (36–41°F).
- Change water every 3–4 days, re-cutting stems each time.
- Strongly scented, so use with caution in corporate/contract work.
- **Form:** Round.

For the Home:

- Re-cut stems and place in clean, fresh water.
- As flowers mature they shed clouds of fine yellow pollen.
- Change water every 3–4 days, re-cutting stems each time.
- Avoid using 'florist's dill' in cooking as flowers may have been treated with chemicals.
- Arrange with lime green roses and grasses for a fresh, summery look.

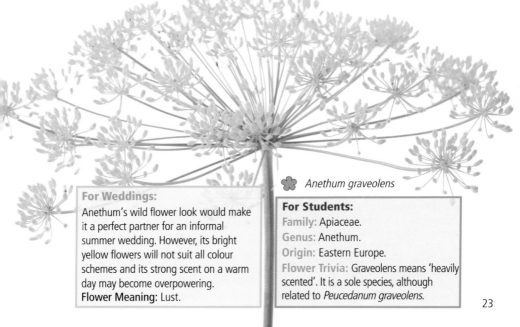

Anethum graveolens

For Weddings:

Anethum's wild flower look would make it a perfect partner for an informal summer wedding. However, its bright yellow flowers will not suit all colour schemes and its strong scent on a warm day may become overpowering.

Flower Meaning: Lust.

For Students:

Family: Apiaceae.
Genus: Anethum.
Origin: Eastern Europe.
Flower Trivia: Graveolens means 'heavily scented'. It is a sole species, although related to *Peucedanum graveolens*.

23

Anigozanthos

Common Name: **Kangaroo paw, Monkey/Cat's paw**

Availability: All year round except for July/August.

Vase Life: Approx 14–21 days.

Flower Notes: Pronounced 'Anni-go-ZANTH-thus'. An unusual shaped tubular flower on a leafless stem whose common name perfectly sums up its appearance. Velvety to look at, it is furry to the touch. Medium stem length.

Colour Range: Fiery colours of orange, red, yellow, green, lime.

For the Florist:

- Ideal temperature range 2–5°C (36–41°F).
- These are thirsty flowers; allow to stand in fresh water for a few hours before using.
- Remove any foliage below the water line, add flower food and change water daily.
- **Form:** Transitional.

For the Home:

- Re-cut stems and place in clean, fresh water which should be changed daily.
- Stems will need to be re-cut regularly to prevent flowers from drying out.
- Benefits from flower food.
- Change water every 2–3 days.
- The tiny hairs can be an irritant to some people, wear gloves if necessary and wash hands after use.

 Anigozanthos 'Yellow Gem'

For Weddings:

Not an obvious candidate for wedding work, unless any of the bridal party is Australian! Use them grouped in modern, structured designs arranged with bold flowers such as Anthuriums and Heliconia. The stems are sturdy enough for wired work.

For Students:

Family: Haemodoraceae.

Genus: Anigozanthos.

Origin: South-west & West Australia.

Flower Trivia: Widely cultivated in Australia, *Anigozanthos manglesii* is the floral emblem of Western Australia.

Anthurium

Common Name: Painter's palette, Tail/Flamingo flower, Hawaiian heart

Availability: All year round.

Vase Life: Approx 14–28 days.

Flower Notes: A very distinctive and popular tropical flower often mistaken as being artificial due to its waxy, almost plastic appearance. Medium stem length.

Colour Range: White, lemon, red, pink, mauve, purple, brown, green; also bicoloured.

For the Florist:

- Optimum temperature 15°C (59°F). Lower temperatures can wilt and blacken the flower.
- Remove plastic phials from stems and re-cut before placing in fresh water.
- Limp flowers can be re-hydrated by misting or submerging in lukewarm water for a few minutes.
- Excess humidity may also damage the flowers.
- Flower food is not necessary.
- **Form:** Round.

For the Home:

- Re-cut stems and place in clean, fresh water. Mist occasionally.
- Keep out of direct heat, draughts and air conditioning.
- Immersing flowers in warm water can increase their vase life.
- Anthuriums exceptional longevity is reduced when arranged in floral foam.
- Arrange Anthuriums with bold flowers such as lilies, Eremurus or Strelitzia.

For Weddings:
Perfect for a contemporary or tropical wedding. Smaller varieties make ideal buttonholes, and you would only need two or three of the larger types in a vase to make an impression. Can also be successfully mixed with more traditional flowers in bridal bouquets.

For Students:
Family: Araceae.
Genus: Anthurium.
Origin: Central and South America.
Flower Trivia: Belonging to the same family as the arum lily, the sap of Anthurium can be an irritant.

Anthurium andraeanum 'Tropical'

Antirrhinum

Common Name: **Snapdragon, Toad's mouth**

Availability: All year round, with different varieties peaking within the year.

Vase Life: Approx 10–14 days.

Flower Notes: Pronounced 'An-ter-RYE-num'. A traditional cottage garden flower with trumpet-shaped flowers on tall spikes. A great favourite with children who like to 'pop' the flowers open. Medium stem length.

Colour Range: White, salmon pink, lavender, bright yellow, orange, red, burgundy. Colours are cheerful often bordering on the fluorescent.

For the Florist:
- Ideal temperature range 1–5°C (34–41°F).
- Store upright to avoid stem curvature.
- Avoid storage in the dark as this may bleach out colour.
- Sensitive to ethylene gas.
- Remove all foliage in contact with water, and change water every 2–3 days, re-cutting stems each time.
- **Form:** Line.

For the Home:
- Re-cut stems every 2–3 days, changing the water each time to extend vase life.
- Remove all foliage in contact with water.
- Remove flower heads as they die. This will encourage upper buds to open.
- Arrange with round-headed summer flowers; *Ammi visnaga*, roses and scabious.

 Antirrhinum majus

For Weddings:
Antirrhinums add valuable height and line to designs, especially pedestal arrangements. Their generally vibrant colour palette may not fit in with more subtle colour schemes, although the white varieties are a popular exception.
Flower Meaning: Gracious lady.

For Students:
Family: Plantaginaceae.
Genus: Antirrhinum.
Origin: Mediterranean.
Flower Trivia: Antirrhinums provide nectar for bumble bees who are one of the few insects that can 'open' the flower.

Aquilegia

Common Name: **Columbine, Granny's bonnet**

Availability: April–May.

Vase Life: Approx 5–7 days.

Flower Notes: Slim, delicate stems support the small, graceful, bell-like flowers of Aquilegia. An old-fashioned cottage garden favourite. Medium stem length.

Colour Range: Pink, purple, crimson, blue, yellow, white.

For the Florist:

- Storage temperature range 2–5°C (36–41°F).
- Avoid lower temperatures as they may cause the flowers to discolour.
- Change water every 2–3 days, re-cutting stems each time and use flower food.
- If Aquilegia arrive 'dry', cut and condition them straightaway, as they wilt quickly when out of water.
- **Form:** Transitional.

For the Home:

- Re-cut stems and place in clean, fresh water with flower food.
- Keep out of draughts and strong sunlight which can cause the flowers to wilt.
- Remove all foliage in contact with water and change water every other day, re-cutting stems each time.
- Arrange with similarly delicate flowers such as stocks, Veronica or spray roses.

 Aquilegia vulgaris

For Weddings:

Aquilegia is an old-fashioned garden flower perfect for a late spring wedding. It would look very pretty in natural country style tied posies although it might get a little lost in large arrangements. If arranging in floral foam, ensure containers are kept topped up with water.
Flower Meaning: Resolved to win.

For Students:

Family: Ranunculaceae.

Genus: Aquilegia

Origin: *Aquilegia vulgaris* from Europe, cultivated varieties from North America.

Flower Trivia: The Rocky Mountain Columbine is the official state flower of Colorado.

Arachnis

Common Name: **Spider/Scorpion orchid**

Availability: Peaks in summer months with limited availability for the rest of the year.

Vase Life: Approx 10–21 days.

Flower Notes: Not dissimilar to a cross between a Dendrobium and a Vanda orchid, these unusual, delicate plants have thick, waxy leaves and fleshy flowers with distinctive divided petals. Between 8–12 heads per stem.

Colour Range: Burgundy, red, gold, burnt orange, often striped.

For the Florist:

- Ideal temperature range 7–15°C (44–60°F).
- Remove any packaging and re-cut stems before placing in water.
- Stand in a light spot, but out of direct heat and away from sources of ethylene gas.
- Mist gently to maintain humidity. Limp flowers can be revived by submerging briefly in tepid water.
- **Form:** Transitional.

For the Home:

- Re-cut stems and stand in clean, fresh water.
- Display at room temperature but away from direct heat which can dry out the flower.
- They prefer a humid atmosphere, mist stems and flowers gently every other day.
- Two or three stems of Arachnis will look stunning arranged in a tall vase with steel or bear grass.

 Arachnis sp.

For Weddings:

This striking orchid will have the most impact when arranged as part of a group of tropical flowers. Equally happy in a vase of water or arranged in floral foam they are also ideal for structured bridal work. Individual heads can be wired or glued for modern corsages and boutonnières.

For Students:

Family: Orchidaceae.

Genus: Arachnis.

Origin: India, S/E Asia and China.

Flower Trivia: Arachnis is a climbing orchid, a thick vine capable of growing more than 5m (15'). Its name comes from Greek for 'spider'.

Asclepias

Common Name: **Orange silk weed, Butterfly weed, Milkweed**

Availability: All year round, peaks June–September.

Vase Life: Approx 7–10 days.

Flower Notes: Pronounced 'Ass-CLAY-pi-ass'. Small but showy flowers are arranged in tight clusters towards the top of a slim stem; slightly untidy in appearance. Medium stem length.

Colour Range: White, orange, yellow, pink, claret.

For the Florist:

- Ideal temperature range 2–4°C (36–39°F).
- Rinse stems before placing in water. Add flower food and change vase water daily.
- Very sensitive to ethylene gas.
- Can be an irritant, wash hands after use.
- **Stem Type:** Latex producing.
- **Form:** Transitional.

For the Home:

- Re-cut stems and remove all foliage in contact with water.
- Add flower food and change water daily.
- Remove flower heads as they die to improve appearance.
- Asclepias exudes a milky sap when cut, rinse thoroughly under a running tap before placing in lukewarm water with flower food.

 Asclepias tuberosa

For Weddings:

Not an obvious choice for a wedding, although it would be a useful filler flower in venue arrangements. It lasts well in floral foam, but its irritant properties make it unsuitable for hand-tied posies. Its vibrant orange colour would complement an autumnal colour scheme.

For Students:

Family: Apocynaceae.

Genus: Asclepias.

Origin: North America.

Flower Trivia: Asclepias is the host plant for the caterpillars of the Monarch butterfly.

Aster (Symphyotrichum)

Common Name: **Michaelmas daisy, September flower**

Availability: All year round.

Vase Life: Approx 7–14 days depending on variety.

Flower Notes: A popular border plant with pyramid-shaped spires of small, delicate daisy-like flowers with wispy foliage. Tall stem length.

Colour Range: White, pink, pale lilac, deep lilac, purple.

For the Florist:

- Ideal temperature range 2–5°C (36–41°F).
- Change water every 2–3 days, re-cutting stems each time and add flower food.
- Remove all foliage in contact with water.
- Display in a cool spot with good air circulation.
- **Form:** Transitional.

For the Home:

- Re-cut stems and place in clean, fresh water.
- Remove all foliage in contact with water.
- Change water every 2–3 days, re-cutting stems each time.
- Flower food is recommended.
- Arrange with more substantial flowers such as Chrysanthemum blooms and roses.

For Weddings:

The delicate shape and pastel shades of Asters make them ideal summer wedding flowers. Suitable for using in water or in floral foam, Aster will add a touch of romantic wispiness to bridal bouquets.
Flower Meaning: Daintiness.

For Students:

Family: Asteraceae.

Genus: Symphyotrichum.

Origin: Northern hemisphere.

Flower Trivia: Previously a member of the Aster genus, Michaelmas daisy has been moved into the genus Symphyotrichum, a change which was adopted by the RHS in 2015.

Symphyotrichum 'Monte Cassino' (Synonym *Aster ericoides*)

Astilbe

Common Name: **False goat's beard, False Spiraea**

Availability: April–November, peaks June–October.

Vase Life: Approx 5–7 days.

Flower Notes: Pronounced 'Ast-STILL-bee'. A popular garden flower with slim stems supporting delicate feathery plumes and attractive dark green spiky foliage. Medium stem length.

Colour Range: Creamy white, pale pink, salmon, dark pink, red.

For the Florist:

- Ideal temperature range 2–5°C (36–41°F).
- Remove all leaves in contact with water and add flower food.
- Sensitive to ethylene gas. Display in an area with good air circulation.
- Astilbe drink a lot of water so check vase levels daily.
- Astilbe exudes a milky sap, rinse off by running stem ends under the tap.
- **Form:** Line.

Astilbe japonica 'Europa Pink'

For the Home:

- Re-cut stems and remove all foliage in contact with water.
- Rinse stem ends thoroughly under running water before placing in a vase and adding flower food.
- Suitable for using in vase designs and floral foam. Astilbe can also be dried by hanging upside down in small bunches in a well-ventilated spot.
- Arrange with more 'solid' flowers, such as scabious and peonies.

For Weddings:

Despite its fragile appearance, Astilbe is a sturdy flower and will add a touch of country chic to arrangements and bouquets. A pretty, delicate flower for summer weddings.

For Students:

Family: Saxifragaceae.

Genus: Astilbe.

Origin: Asia and North America.

Flower Trivia: : The National Collection of Astilbe is held by the Lakeland Horticultural Society at Holehird Gardens, Cumbria.

Astrantia

Common Name: **Great masterwort, Hattie's pincushion**

Availability: From March–November, peaks May–October.

Vase Life: Approx 5–10 days.

Flower Notes: A very pretty, delicate star-shaped flower on branched wiry stems with an almost straw-like feel to the touch. A cottage garden favourite, it also grows in the wild. Medium stem length.

Colour Range: Creamy white, pale pink, dark pink, burgundy.

For the Florist:

- Ideal temperature range 8–10°C (46–50°F).
- Never leave out of water, and always add flower food.
- Remove all leaves in contact with water.
- **Stem Type:** Hollow.
- **Form:** Transitional.

For the Home:

- Re-cut stems and place in clean, fresh water.
- Benefits from using flower food.
- Heads can shatter easily, handle with care.
- Easy to dry by hanging bunches upside down in a cool, well-ventilated spot.
- Arrange with delicate summer flowers such as stocks, Nigella or spray roses.

 Astrantia major 'Roma'

For Weddings:

A lovely, textural flower, ideal for spring and summer weddings, especially in tied posies and particularly good for brides going for a very natural look.
Can be used in both vase designs and arrangements. Suitable for wiring into buttonholes and corsages.

For Students:

Family: Apiaceae.
Genus: Astrantia.
Origin: Europe and Western Asia.
Flower Trivia: An old, well established flower, Astrantia was first cultivated in Britain in the 16th century, reaching America 100 years later.

Banksia

Common Name: **Acorn Banksia, Australian honeysuckle**

Availability: April–December.

Vase Life: 7–14 days.

Flower Notes: An Australian native flower which looks not unlike a large, furry microphone. Very solid and dense to the touch, it has a wool-like texture. Medium stem length.

Colour Range: Cream, yellow, red/orange.

🌸 🌸 *Banksia hookeriana*

For the Florist:

- Ideal temperature range 5–8°C (41–46°F).
- Needs good air circulation to prevent the flowers from becoming mouldy.
- These are thirsty flowers, so check vase levels regularly.
- Prefers cool conditions.
- Woody stemmed, cut with secateurs.
- **Form:** Round.

For the Home:

- Re-cut stems with secateurs and place in clean, fresh water.
- Avoid getting the flowers wet, as this can cause black streaks.
- If using in floral foam, they need to be well anchored in as they can be top heavy.
- Banksia can be dried easily. Simply stand them in a vase without any water in a cool place. Drying should take about 3 weeks.

For Weddings:

If a bride is going for a tropical theme, then Banksia would certainly make an impression! Use grouped and low down in church and reception designs for maximum impact. Their soft furry look gives them a certain appeal for Christmas and winter arrangements.

For Students:

Family: Proteaceae.

Genus: Banksia.

Origin: Australia and Tasmania.

Flower Trivia: The flower is named after Sir Joseph Banks, who on Cook's voyage of 1770, was the first European to collect Banksia specimens.

33

Bouvardia

Common Name: **Bouvardia**

Availability: All year round.

Vase Life: Approx 7–14 days.

Flower Notes: A delicate, hothouse plant of small, star-shaped flowers in both single and double forms borne in clusters at the top of the stem. Long stem length.

Colour Range: White, cream, pale pink, dark pink, salmon, red.

For the Florist:

- Ideal temperature range 2–10°C (36–50°F). Lower temperatures may cause the flowers to wilt.
- Remove excess foliage and re-cut stems, removing any white ends.
- Prone to water loss and sensitive to ethylene gas.
- Re-cut stems every 2–3 days to keep in top condition, changing the water each time.
- Use specialist flower food if provided, reducing its use in winter.
- **Form:** Transitional.

For the Home:

- Re-cut stems at an angle and place in clean, fresh water.
- Remove all foliage in contact with water, re-cutting stems every 2–3 days.
- Arrange in tall vases with roses or peonies. Bouvardia does not last well in floral foam.

For Weddings:

A very pretty flower to use in bridal work, adding a soft, feminine touch to both tied posies and vase designs. The subtlety of the flowers may get a little lost in large flamboyant arrangements. Not suitable for wired work.

Flower meaning: Enthusiasm.

For Students:

Family: Rubiaceae

Genus: Bouvardia.

Origin: Tropical America and Mexico.

Flower Trivia: Named after Parisian doctor Charles Bouvard, personal physician to Louis XIII, and director of the Jardin des Plantes in Paris.

Bouvardia longiflora 'Diamond Pink'

Brassica

Common Name: **Ornamental cabbage**

Availability: July–February, peaks September–January.

Vase Life: Approx 7–10 days.

Flower Notes: Guaranteed to raise an eyebrow as a cut flower, ornamental cabbage will also add a splash of vibrant colour and texture to bouquets and arrangements. Not everyone's choice however! Medium stem length.

Colour Range: Cream, green, purple, pink, aubergine.

For the Florist:

- Ideal temperature range 2–10°C (36–50°F) although reasonably resistant to low temperatures.
- Brassica's thick stem can dehydrate quickly if left out of water.
- Cut approx. 5cm/2" from the bottom of the stem at an angle to encourage water uptake.
- Benefits from flower food.
- **Form:** Round.

For the Home:

- Re-cut stems at an angle and place in clean, fresh water.
- To avoid any cabbage odours, change water every 2–3 days and remove any yellowing leaves.
- Keep out of direct sunlight.
- However attractive the flower, ornamental cabbages are not for eating.
- Suitable for vase designs or for arranging in floral foam.

Brassica oleracea 'Rose Crane'

For Weddings:

Although a cabbage would not be most peoples' idea for a wedding flower, they are a popular choice for many modern designers. A bride keen on gardening or with a farming background (and a sense of humour) might appreciate them - they would certainly be a talking point!

For Students:

Family: Brassicaceae.

Genus: Brassica.

Origin: Western Europe, Mediterranean and temperate regions of Asia.

Flower Trivia: Member of the mustard family which also includes broccoli, Brussel sprouts and turnip.

35

Bupleurum

Common Name: **Thorow-wax, Hare's ear**

Availability: May–December, peaks June–November.

Vase Life: Approx 8–14 days.

Flower Notes: Pronounced 'Boo-PLEUR-rum'. A delicate filler flower made up of tiny star-shaped flowers which are widely used as a medicinal herb, particularly in Chinese medicine where it is known as Chai Hu. Medium stem length.

Colour Range: Lime green teamed with acid yellow.

For the Florist:

- Ideal temperature range 2–5°C (36–41°F).
- Stems are delicate, so handle with care.
- Re-cut stems every 3–4 days, changing water each time.
- A thirsty flower, keep vases topped up and add flower food.
- **Form:** Transitional.

For the Home:

- Re-cut stems at an angle and place in clean, fresh water.
- Remove all foliage in contact with water, and add flower food.
- If stems become tangled, hold them upside down and gently pull apart.
- Change vase water every 3–4 days, re-cutting stems each time.
- Use to complement bolder flowers such as roses, Gerberas or scabious.

 Bupleurum griffithii

For Weddings:

Use the tiny yellow/lime flowers of Bupleurum to set off more intense, jewel like colours such as cerise pinks and deep purples; it will also lift the more neutral shades of creams and lemons.
An excellent filler flower in large arrangements and vases, it can also be wired for buttonholes and corsages.

For Students:

Family: Apiaceae.

Genus: Bupleurum.

Origin: Asia.

Flower Trivia: The common name thorow-wax is a corruption of 'through-grow' as the stems of the flowers appear to emerge from the leaves.

Calendula

Common Name: **English/Pot marigold**

Availability: May–July.

Vase Life: Approx 5–7 days.

Flower Notes: Cheerful, double flowering Calendula is also grown as an annual border plant and is a familiar sight in gardens in the summer. There is a slightly spicy, peppery smell to the leaves. Medium stem length.

Colour Range: Bright orange, sunny yellow.

For the Florist:

- Ideal temperature range 2–5°C (36–41°F).
- Display in shallow water which should be changed every other day.
- Will benefit from using flower food.
- Form: Round.

For the Home:

- Re-cut stems at an angle and place in clean, fresh water.
- Remove all foliage in contact with water.
- Avoid humid conditions and direct sunlight.
- Calendula will last longer as a cut flower in water than arranged in floral foam.

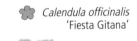 *Calendula officinalis* 'Fiesta Gitana'

For Weddings:

These sunny flowers would look just the part tied into simple bunches and popped into rustic-style containers for a summer wedding with a vintage theme. Temper their vivid colours with soft creams and lemons or fire them up with hot shades of reds and burnt orange. Not suitable for wired work.

For Students:

Family: Asteraceae.

Genus: Calendula.

Origin: Southern Europe and Iran.

Flower Trivia: Despite its common name, Calendula is not related to the marigold. It is used extensively in herbal medicine, particularly in skin products.

Callicarpa

Common Name: **Beautyberry, Murasaki Shikibu**

Availability: August–December, peaks September–November.

Vase Life: Approx 10–14 days.

Flower Notes: An ornamental garden shrub, sporting bead-like clusters of berries with a metallic lustre appearing on bare branches in the autumn and winter. Medium stem length.

Colour Range: Rich violet.

For the Florist:

- Ideal temperature range 0–2°C (32–36°F).
- Prefers cool temperatures, display away from direct heat sources.
- Re-cut stems with secateurs every 3–4 days, changing water each time.
- **Stem Type:** Woody, use secateurs.
- **Form:** Transitional.

For the Home:

- Re-cut stems with secateurs and place in clean, fresh water.
- To prolong vase life, display out of direct heat sources.
- Change water every 3–4 days, re-cutting stems each time.
- Mist occasionally to prevent berry drop.
- Arrange with strong, bold flowers such as Dahlias, Gerberas and lilies.

 Callicarpa bodinieri var. *giraldii*

For Weddings:

A rich, unusual coloured berry which would look very effective contrasted with deep reds and oranges. Use it to accentuate the rich colours of autumn and winter weddings, where its leafless branches would stand out in more structured designs. Cut into small lengths, it can be used in wired work.

For Students:

Family: Lamiaceae.

Genus: Callicarpa.

Origin: Eastern Asia, Australia, North & Central America.

Flower Trivia: Murasaki Shikibu was a Japanese novelist and poet, author of 'The Tale of Genji', one of the earliest novels in human history.

Callistephus

Common Name: **China aster, Matsumoto aster**

Availability: April–September.

Vase Life: Approx 7–10 days.

Flower Notes: An old-fashioned cottage garden flower with strong autumnal associations. The bushy, daisy-like flower head can be in both single and double forms. Short/medium stem length.

Colour Range: Rich purple, lilac, crimson, pink, white, yellow.

For the Florist:

- Ideal temperature range 2–10°C (36–50°F).
- Use flower food to prevent the stems from polluting the water.
- Change water every other day, re-cutting stems each time.
- Handle with care as flowers can be top heavy and break easily.
- **Form:** Round.

For the Home:

- Re-cut stems at an angle and place in clean, fresh water.
- Remove all foliage in contact with water.
- Warm conditions can cause the stems to pollute vase water.
- Add flower food to the water, which should be changed every other day, re-cutting stems each time.
- Arrange with textured Amaranthus, Dahlias or Hypericum berries.

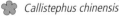 *Callistephus chinensis*

For Weddings:

The rich colours of Callistephus will add warmth and charm to autumn weddings. More suitable arranged in water than in floral foam, they would be ideal for hand-held posies. Tie with raffia and pop into a simple container for a touch of rustic chic.

Flower meaning: Fidelity.

For Students:

Family: Asteraceae.

Genus: Callistephus.

Origin: Native to East Asia.

Flower Trivia: Very popular as a cut flower in Japan, Callistephus was first brought to Europe in the 1790's.

Calluna

Common Name: **Heather, Ling**

Availability: In flower, July–October, all year as an evergreen.

Vase Life: Approx 6–10 days.

Flower Notes: A low growing perennial shrub, common on acidic soils and usually found on heaths and moorland, although it is also very popular in gardens and landscaping schemes. Short stem length.

Colour Range: White, mauve, pink, lavender, red.

For the Florist:

- Ideal temperature range 2–5°C (36–41°F).
- Woody stemmed – cut with secateurs.
- Display out of direct heat and draughts which can cause flowers to drop.
- Don't overcrowd buckets or containers, and change water frequently.
- **Form:** Transitional.

For the Home:

- Re-cut stems and stand in clean, fresh water removing any foliage below the water line.
- Display at room temperature but away from direct heat which can dry out the flower.
- Heathers are thirsty flowers – keep vase levels topped up.
- Will add texture and character to autumn flowers and berries.

 Calluna vulgaris

For Weddings:

The first candidate for a Scottish wedding! A lovely textured flower for using in bridal designs, but not suitable for larger, more flamboyant arrangements. Ideal for wiring, as it is sturdy and will withstand handling. Ideal for late summer, early autumn weddings. Use a plant if cut heather is unavailable.

Flower meaning: Protection.

For Students:

Family: Ericaceae.

Genus: Calluna.

Origin: Europe, Asia Minor, N/W Africa.

Flower Trivia: Traditionally used in making besoms, as mentioned in the 18th century folk song 'Buy Broom Buzzems' attributed to Blind Willie.

Campanula

Common Name: **Bellflower, Canterbury bells, Harebell, Cup & saucer**

Availability: April–September.

Vase Life: Approx 7–10 days.

Flower Notes: A quintessential cottage garden plant most commonly recognised as bell-shaped flowers on tall stems. A native wild flower in the UK. Medium to tall stem length.

Colour Range: White, pale pink, lilac, lavender, pale blue, deep blue.

For the Florist:

- Ideal temperature range 2–5°C (36–41°F).
- Re-cut stems and remove foliage in contact with water.
- Change water every 2–3 days, re-cutting stems each time and add flower food.
- Form: Line.

For the Home:

- Re-cut stems at an angle and place in clean, fresh water with flower food.
- Remove all foliage in contact with water and change water every other day, re-cutting stems each time.
- Campanulas are delicate flowers, so handle with care.
- Arrange with pastel summery flowers such as scabious and Nigella.

 Campanula 'Champion Pink'

For Weddings:
The delicate shades of Campanula would complement a pastel colour scheme, and would be ideal for an extravagant floral summer wedding. Perfect for large pedestal arrangements and vase designs. One of its many common names is fairy thimbles, which could make Campanula the ultimate fairytale wedding flower!

Flower meaning: Gratitude.

For Students:
Family: Campanulaceae.

Genus: Campanula.

Origin: Widely distributed across the northern hemisphere.

Flower Trivia: In Germany and the Netherlands Campanula is known as 'Rapunzel Bellflower' and supposedly was the inspiration behind Grimm's fairy tale.

Carthamus

Common Name: **Safflower**

Availability: April–December, peaks June–October.

Vase Life: Approx 7–10 days.

Flower Notes: Resembling a fluffy orange thistle, Carthamus is a cheerful herbaceous plant, also popular as a dried flower. It has strong autumnal associations. Medium/tall stem length.

Colour Range: Vivid orange, yellow.

For the Florist:

- Ideal temperature range 2–4°C (36–39°F).
- Needs good air circulation to stop the flowers from going mouldy.
- Keep away from excess heat and draughts.
- Remove foliage in contact with water and change water every 2–3 days re-cutting stems each time.
- **Form:** Transitional.

For the Home:

- Re-cut stems at an angle and place in clean, fresh water.
- Remove any foliage in contact with water and change water every other day, re-cutting stems each time.
- Any unopened green buds will not open further.
- Flowers and stems can be prickly to the touch.
- Dry by hanging upside down in bunches in a cool, dark, well-ventilated spot.

For Weddings:

Carthamus is not really pretty enough for bridal work, but would be a useful filler flower for large arrangements in churches and venues, particularly for autumn weddings. The green unopened buds will add an interesting texture to wired designs.

For Students:

Family: Asteraceae.

Genus: Carthamus.

Origin: Eastern Mediterranean.

Flower Trivia: Traditionally used for making dyes, its seeds are sometimes used in bird feeders as squirrels dislike the taste!

Carthamus tinctorius 'Kinko'

Celosia

Availability: March–December, peaks May–November.

Vase Life: Approx 5–6 days.

Flower Notes: A tender annual from tropical regions, *C. argentea* is a singular looking flower which grows in a range of bright, vibrant colours. It is soft and velvety to the touch. Medium stem length.

Colour Range: Bright pink, red, yellow, orange and green.

For the Florist:

- Ideal temperature range 5–8°C (41–46°F).
- Prone to drooping, this flower needs good air circulation and careful handling.
- Leave out of cooler once conditioned to avoid fungal growth as flowers are susceptible to botrytis.
- Change water daily, adding flower food and re-cutting stems each time.
- **Form:** Line.

For the Home:

- Re-cut stems and place in clean, fresh water which should be changed daily.
- Remove all foliage above and below water level and add flower food.
- Display out of direct heat and draughts.
- Arrange with textural flowers such as large headed Chrysanthemums, Hypericum and Dahlias.

For Weddings:

The rich colours of Celosia will add vibrancy and texture to tied bridal designs, however its soft stem makes it unsuitable for using in floral foam. Consider this interesting flower for an autumn wedding, especially when grouped with berries and similarly brightly coloured flowers and foliage. Not suitable for wiring.

 Celosia argentea var. *cristata*

For Students:

Family: Amaranthaceae.

Genus: Celosia.

Origin: Tropical regions.

Flower Trivia: A great flower to grow in your garden if you want to attract bees and butterflies. In warmer climates they are great favourites of hummingbirds.

43

Celosia

Common Name: **Cockscomb**

Availability: May–November, peaks June–November.

Vase Life: Approx 5–6 days.

Flower Notes: A very unusual flower, not dissimilar to coral in appearance, or, as described by some, brain-shaped. In a range of fabulous colours with contrasting bright green foliage. Medium stem length.

Colour Range: Jewel colours of burgundy, cerise pink, red, yellow, orange and green.

For the Florist:

- Ideal temperature range 5–8°C (41–46°F).
- Remove excess foliage to prevent flowers from drying out.
- Susceptible to botrytis, so leave out of cooler once conditioned to avoid fungal growth.
- Needs good air circulation, remove from wrappers to condition and don't overcrowd vases.
- **Form:** Round.

For the Home:

- Re-cut stems and place in clean, fresh water.
- Remove all foliage above and below water level and add flower food.
- Display out of direct heat, and refresh water daily.
- Arrange with round flowers such as sunflowers and carnations for contrast.

 Celosia cristata

For Weddings:
Not a flower commonly associated with weddings, although it would add lovely contrast and texture to tied bridal designs. Great for adding into vases, not so good in floral foam as the stems are quite soft. An autumn bride would appreciate them when grouped with berries and grasses.

For Students:
Family: Amaranthaceae.
Genus: Celosia.
Origin: Tropical regions.
Flower Trivia: The name comes from the Greek word for 'burnt' a reference to the fiery colours and shape of this unusual flower.

Centaurea

Common Name: **Cornflower, Bachelor's button, Bluebottle**

Availability: May–October.

Vase Life: Approx 5–7 days.

Flower Notes: Fragile and delicate, the soft, tiny petals have an almost thistle-like appearance. Once common in the countryside, wild cornflowers are now classified as an endangered species. Short stem length.

Colour Range: Brilliant blue, maroon, pink, white.

For the Florist:

- Ideal temperature range: 2–5°C (36–41°F).
- Needs good air circulation, as cornflowers are sensitive to ethylene gas.
- Remove all foliage in contact with water and add flower food.
- Keep vases topped up as these are thirsty flowers!
- **Stem Type:** Soft.

For the Home:

- Re-cut stems and place in clean, fresh water with flower food.
- Remove all foliage in contact with water and change water every other day.
- Perfect for vases, but stems are not strong enough to be used in floral foam.
- To dry cornflowers, they need to be very fresh, else the petals will drop. Air dry them by hanging them upside down in a cool, airy place.
- Arrange with delicate summer flowers such as larkspur, pinks or Nigella.

 Centaurea cyanus

For Weddings:

A gorgeous summer wedding flower, particularly for brides keen on achieving a natural, wild flower effect. Use in tied posies where they will complement soft pink and pastel shades. Cornflower stems are too soft for wiring, but individual heads can be glued with care.

Flower meaning: Delicacy.

For Students:

Family: Asteraceae.

Genus: Centaurea.

Origin: Native to Europe.

Flower Trivia: The national flower of Estonia, Centaurea is also one of the ingredients in Twining's Lady Gray Tea.

Cestrum

Common Name: **Jessamine**

Availability: October–May.

Vase Life: Approx 10–14 days.

Flower Notes: A bushy flower on a sturdy stem, Cestrum is long lasting and good value for money. Not a common cut flower, the fragrant Cestrum is more popular as a garden shrub. Medium stem length.

Colour Range: Pinky red, rose, sulphur yellow.

For the Florist:

- Ideal temperature range 2–8°C (36–46°F).
- Remove all foliage in contact with water and add flower food.
- Change water every 4–5 days, re-cutting the stems each time.
- **Form:** Line.

For the Home:

- Re-cut stems at an angle and place in clean, fresh water with flower food.
- Remove all foliage in contact with water and change water every 2–3 days.
- Arrange with tall flowers such as gladioli and showy Chrysanthemum blooms.
- Wash hands after use.

 *Cestrum* 'Red Zohar'

For Weddings:

Cestrum would make a good filler flower for showy church and reception arrangements. Its colour range, although limited, would complement an autumnal wedding colour scheme. As it has a toxic quality, it's probably best avoided in tied designs and wired work.

For Students:

Family: Solanaceae.

Genus: Cestrum.

Origin: Central & South America.

Flower Trivia: Popular with some species of butterfly, who are able to neutralise the toxins within the plant making themselves noxious in turn to any would-be predators.

Chamelaucium

Common Name: **Waxflower, Geraldton wax**

Availability: October–May, peaks November–April.

Vase Life: Approx 10–14 days.

Flower Notes: Pronounced 'Sham-a LAW-see-um'. A robust shrub, its common name comes from the waxy appearance of its tiny, numerous flowers. Very useful as a filler flower, some varieties have a slight lemon scent. Medium stem length.

Colour Range: Creamy white, pale pink, deep pink. Occasionally dyed in other shades.

For the Florist:

- Ideal temperature range 2–8°C (36–46°F).
- Susceptible to ethylene gas and botrytis which can eat away at the petals.
- Change water every 2–3 days re-cutting stems each time.
  Display in an area with good air circulation to avoid foliage drop.
- Cooler temperatures will prolong its vase life.
- **Stem Type:** Woody stemmed, cut with secateurs.
- **Form:** Transitional.

For the Home:

- Re-cut stems with secateurs and place in clean, fresh water.
- Flower food is not necessary - it encourages nectar production which makes the flowers sticky.
- Lasts well in floral foam but don't mist flowers as dampness can cause mould.
- Cut into small pieces Chamelaucium looks very pretty arranged with spring flowers such as tulips or Ranunculus.

 Chamelaucium uncinatum 'Snowflake'

For Weddings:

The delicate appearance and soft shades of waxflower make it ideal for softening the outline of tied posies. It is not that dissimilar in appearance to rosemary so would be a useful flower for brides who are looking for a natural combination of flowers and herbs.

For Students:

Family: Myrtaceae.

Genus: Chamelaucium.

Origin: Western Australia.

Flower Trivia: The common name Geraldton wax is a reference to Geraldton in Perth, Western Australia, where it grows in the wild in large numbers.

Chelone

Common Name: **Pink turtlehead**

Availability: July–September.

Vase Life: Approx 10–14 days.

Flower Notes: A cultivated wild flower from North America, Chelone is a robust perennial with a strong, sturdy stem and attractive lance-shaped leaves. Medium stem length.

Colour Range: Purplish pink.

For the Florist:

- Ideal temperature range 2–8°C (36–46°F).
- Remove all foliage in contact with water and add flower food.
- Change water every 4–5 days, re-cutting stems each time.
- Form: Line.

For the Home:

- Re-cut stems and place in clean, fresh water with flower food.
- Check water level in vase and change water every 3–4 days, re-cutting stems each time.
- Its sturdiness and long vase life makes it an excellent cut flower.
- Arrange with summery flowers: Phlox, scabious and spray roses.

Chelone obliqua

For Weddings:

Although not a common choice for bridal flowers, Chelone is reliable and adaptable and would complement a summery colour range as well as making an interesting addition to church and reception arrangements. Not suitable for wired work.

For Students:

Family: Plantaginaceae.

Genus: Chelone.

Origin: Native to eastern North America.

Flower Trivia: Chelone grows naturally in the wild on the banks of streams and in boggy meadows in the United States.

Chrysanthemum (Bloom)

Common Name: **Bloom, Spider bloom, Pompon**

Availability: All year round.

Vase Life: Approx 14–21 days.

Flower Notes: A showy, unmistakable flower, seen as a little old-fashioned by some although the 'spider' bloom with its spiky petals has a certain retro appeal. Tall stem length.

Colour Range: White, cream, yellow, lime green, mauve, pink, tawny orange.

For the Florist:

- Ideal temperature range 8–10°C (46–50°F).
- Plastic bags protecting the heads can be removed more easily if sprayed with water first.
- A clean vase and fresh water is essential for maximum vase life.
- Change vase water every 3–4 days, re-cutting stems each time.
- Allow flowers to have a long drink of cold water before using.
- Form: Round.

Chrysanthemum 'Kiev'

For the Home:

- Re-cut stems and place in clean, fresh water with flower food.
- Remove all foliage in contact with water and change water every 3–4 days, re-cutting stems each time.
- Handle with care, as the heads can shatter easily.
- Displaying in deep water will help to stop leaves from drooping.
- Team with tall, bold flowers, such as gladioli and lilies.

Chrysanthemum 'Anastasia Lime'

For Weddings:
The heads are a little too large for bridal flowers, but they are a flowery and flamboyant must for church or cathedral weddings, especially in the autumn. A single bloom would make a wonderfully over-the-top buttonhole, but handle with care!

For Students:
Family: Asteraceae.
Genus: Chrysanthemum.
Origin: Asia and N/E Europe.
Flower Trivia: Chrysanthemum tea, a popular herbal drink in China, is thought to decrease body heat and is used in the treatment of fevers.

49

Chrysanthemum (Spray)

Common Name: **Xanth, Mum, Buttons, AYR (All-year-round)**

Availability: All year round.

Vase Life: Approx 14–21 days.

Flower Notes: The Chrysanthemum often receives a rather bad press which is largely undeserved. Extremely versatile and with vastly improved varieties now available, Chrysanthemum is both a useful and reliable flower. Medium stem length.

Colour Range: A vast range of colours including a striking lime green, no blue however!

For the Florist:

- Ideal temperature range 2–8°C (36–46°F).
- Make sure all buckets are clean and don't overcrowd the flowers. Remove any foliage in contact with water.
- Re-cut stems and change water every 4–5 days, adding flower food each time.
- They emit large amounts of ethylene gas, so keep away from ethylene sensitive flowers.
- **Form:** Transitional.

For the Home:

- Re-cut stems and place in clean, fresh water with flower food.
- Remove all foliage in contact with water and change water every 4–5 days.
- When fresh, the flowers will have a hard, tight centre, which will soften as the flower matures.
- The leaves will turn yellow and wilt before the flowers die.

Chrysanthemum
'Tiger Rag'

For Weddings:
Although unlikely to make its way into your average bridal bouquet, the Chrysanthemum should not be underestimated for its versatility and value in church and reception arrangements. The single white varieties are a useful substitute for brides looking for 'daisys' in their bouquets.
Flower meaning: Abundance & wealth.

For Students:
Family: Asteraceae.
Genus: Chrysanthemum.
Origin: Asia and N/E Europe.
Flower Trivia: The national flower of Japan, the 9th of September is Chrysanthemum Day, also known as the Festival of Happiness.

Cirsium

Common Name: **Thistle, Plume thistle**

Availability: July–September.

Vase Life: Approx 7 – 10 days.

Flower Notes: Pronounced 'Sir-see-um'. A deciduous, upright perennial with branching stems and soft, fluffy flowers. Growing as a 'weed' in the wild, there are cultivated varieties for the garden and the cut flower market. Medium stem length.

Colour Range: Pinky mauve.

For the Florist:

- Ideal temperature range 2–5°C (36–41°F).
- Display out of direct heat and draughts.
- Needs good air circulation, sensitive to ethylene gas.
- Don't overcrowd buckets or containers, and change water frequently.
- **Form:** Round.

For the Home:

- Re-cut stems and stand in clean, fresh water removing any foliage below water line.
- Display at room temperature but away from direct heat sources.
- A non-prickly variety is grown for arranging!
- This pretty 'wild flower' will look lovely arranged simply with cornflowers and *Alchemilla mollis*.

Cirsium 'Pink Beauty'

For Weddings:

A lovely flower, in tune with the trend for the natural 'just picked' look and, of course, perfect for a Scottish wedding. Ideal for tied bridal posies where it would add contrast and texture, but may get a little lost in larger designs. Can be used in floral foam, but is happier in a vase. Can be wired, but only with care as it doesn't last very well out of water.

Flower meaning: Nobility.

For Students:

Family: Asteraceae.

Genus: Cirsium.

Origin: Eurasia, N. Africa.

Flower Trivia: The flower of Scotland, the thistle was also the emblem of the Encyclopaedia Britannica, first published in Edinburgh in 1768.

51

Clarkia

Common Name: **Godetia, Satin flower, Farewell to spring**

Availability: May–August.

Vase Life: Approx 7–10 days.

Flower Notes: A garden annual with funnel-shaped, papery petals which are borne in clusters at the top of slim stems with strap-like leaves. Medium stem length.

Colour Range: White, salmon, pale pink, cerise pink.

For the Florist:

- Ideal temperature range 2–5°C (36–41°F).
- Lower temperatures can cause the flowers to turn transparent.
- Change water every 2–3 days re-cutting stems each time and add flower food.
- Display in a cool spot out of sunlight and direct heat sources.
- **Stem Type:** Hollow.
- **Form:** Transitional.

For the Home:

- Re-cut stems and stand in clean, fresh water.
- Add flower food and change water every 2–3 days re-cutting stems each time.
- Stand in a cool spot with good air circulation.
- For a country garden look, arrange Clarkia with Ageratum and Sweet William.

For Weddings:
Clarkia would make a very pretty addition to hand-tied posies and shower bouquets. Its stems are strong enough to use in floral foam, and individual flower heads can be wired for corsages.

Flower meaning: Sincerity.

Clarkia amoena 'Grace White'

For Students:
Family: Onagraceae.

Genus: Clarkia.

Origin: North America.

Flower Trivia: Clarkia was named after the American explorer, Captain William Clarke who identified the flower during an expedition to the Pacific coast.

Clematis

Common Name: **Virgin's bower, Vase vine, Old man's beard**

Availability: All year round, peaks September–January.

Vase Life: Approx 5–7 days.

Flower Notes: A popular climbing plant with showy, cup-shaped flowers and attractive buds and foliage. Clematis has only recently become commercially available as a cut flower. Medium stem length.

Colour Range: Violet blue, crimson.

For the Florist:

● Ideal temperature range 5–8°C (41–46°F).

● Re-cut stems every other day to aid water uptake and mist frequently.

● Display out of direct heat and draughts which will dehydrate the flower.

● Handle carefully as stems can easily tangle.

● **Form:** Transitional.

For the Home:

● Re-cut stems and place in clean, fresh water.

● Keep out of direct heat and draughts.

● Revive drooping flowers by re-cutting stems and spraying lightly with water.

● Perfect for vases, but will only last 2–3 days in floral foam.

● Arrange with equally gorgeous summer flowers such as peonies, roses and Delphiniums.

 Clematis 'Blue Pirouette'

For Weddings:

Clematis would be a lovely flower to include in bridal designs, its trailing habit making it perfect for shower bouquets in particular. It would look fantastic in late summer weddings, and the feathery seed heads which follow the flowers would be perfect for autumn wedding work.

Flower meaning: Ingenuity.

For Students:

Family: Ranunculaceae.

Genus: Clematis.

Origin: Native to many countries although a large majority of Clematis species originate from China.

Flower Trivia: Pioneers of the American Old West called Clematis 'pepper vine' and used it to spice up food.

Consolida

Common Name: **Larkspur**

Availability: June–October, peaks June–August.

Vase Life: Approx 7–10 days.

Flower Notes: An old-fashioned cottage garden plant, closely related to Delphinium with tall spires of soft-hued, double flowers and wispy foliage. Medium stem length.

Colour Range: Creamy white, pale pink, lilac, pale blue, purple.

For the Florist:

- Ideal temperature range 2–5°C (36–41°F).
- Don't overcrowd flowers, they need good air circulation to prevent flower drop.
- Remove all foliage in contact with water to prevent slime forming.
- Change water daily and ensure buckets and vases are kept clean.
- **Stem Type:** Hollow.
- **Form:** Line.

For the Home:

- Re-cut stems and place in clean, fresh water with flower food.
- Remove all foliage in contact with water and change water every other day re-cutting stems each time.
- The flowers will drop if the stems are allowed to dry out.
- Larkspur can be dried by hanging bunches upside down in a cool, dry place with good air circulation.
- Arrange with Nigella, scabious or Bouvardia for a vase of true summer flowers.

Consolida ajacis

For Weddings:

Larkspur can be used in tied posies, but its delicate linear form makes it ideal for shower bouquets. Equally versatile in floral foam or water, larkspur is perfect for brides looking for a pretty, summer wedding flower. Dried larkspur petals make great confetti.

Flower meaning: An open heart.

For Students:

Family: Ranunculaceae.

Genus: Consolida.

Origin: Mediterranean & West Asia.

Flower Trivia: Larkspur is a member of the buttercup family; its common name derives from the distinctive shape of its flowers.

Convallaria

Common Name: **Lily of the valley, Our Lady's tears**

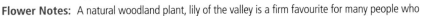

Availability: March–May.

Vase Life: Approx 4–6 days.

Flower Notes: A natural woodland plant, lily of the valley is a firm favourite for many people who love its sweet fragrance and pretty, delicate bell-like flowers. Short stem length.

Colour Range: Ivory white, pale rose pink.

For the Florist:

- Flowers attached to their rhizomes can be left dry initially at temperatures of 0–1°C (32–34°F).
- Once cut the ideal temperature range is 2–3°C (36–38°F).
- They are thirsty flowers; stand in clean, fresh water which should be changed daily. Add flower food.
- Revive limp flowers by submerging in cold water for approx. 1 hr.
- Mist occasionally and display in a cool spot with good air circulation.
- Soft stemmed and delicate, handle with care.
- **Form:** Line.

For the Home:

- Re-cut stems and place in clean, fresh water with flower food.
- Display in a cool spot and mist occasionally with cold water.
- Keep out of direct heat sources and sunlight.
- Lily of the valley lasts longer in water than in floral foam.

For Weddings:

A beautiful and dainty wedding flower, ideal for delicate hand-tied posies and bridal bouquets, although it can dry out quickly if arranged in floral foam. It can be used with care in wired work, but may wilt in the heat on a sunny day.

Flower meaning: Happiness.

For Students:

Family: Asparagaceae.

Genus: Convallaria.

Origin: Northern hemisphere.

Flower Trivia: 'Muguets des bois' is sold traditionally on the streets of France on May 1st.

Convallaria majalis

55

Cosmos

Common Name: **Chocolate Cosmos, Mexican aster**

Availability: June–October.

Vase Life: Approx 4–6 days.

Flower Notes: A fashionable garden plant with a single, daisy-like flower on a tall leafless stem with papery-thin petals. The variety *Cosmos atrosanguineus* smells faintly of chocolate. Medium stem length.

Colour Range: White, brownish red, pink.

For the Florist:

- Ideal temperature range 2–5°C (36–41°F).
- Keep out of draughts and direct heat.
- Display in fresh, cold water which should be changed daily, and add flower food.
- Handle with care as stems can become easily tangled.
- **Stem Type:** Soft.

For the Home:

- Re-cut stems and place in clean, fresh water with flower food.
- Warm conditions will shorten its vase life, display in a cool spot.
- The scent of chocolate will become stronger as the day wears on.
- Arrange with the autumnal shades of Crocosmia, Dahlia and Amaranthus.

For Weddings:
The rich colour of Cosmos will contrast beautifully with dusky pinks and will complement rich autumn shades of golds and reds. They are ideal for creating pretty tied posies and vintage-style vase designs, although a little too delicate for wired work and for using in floral foam.

For Students:
Family: Asteraceae.
Genus: Cosmos.
Origin: Native to Mexico.
Flower Trivia: The distinctive scent of Cosmos is due to an organic compound called vanillin, which the Aztecs used as flavouring for chocolate. Cosmos is now extinct as a wild flower in Mexico.

 Cosmos atrosanguineus

Craspedia

Availability: All year round.

Vase Life: Approx 10–14 days.

Flower Notes: An unusual perennial consisting of a single, solid globe of tightly-packed flowers on a leafless stem. Medium stem length.

Colour Range: Mustard yellow.

For the Florist:

- Ideal temperature range 2–5°C (36–41°F).
- Display in an area with good air circulation, this will help to prevent the stems from turning black.
- Change water every 3–4 days and add flower food.
- **Form:** Round.

For the Home:

- Re-cut stems and place in clean, fresh water.
- Use flower food and change water every 3–4 days.
- Craspedia has more impact grouped rather than arranged singly.
- The flower will shed fine yellow pollen as it matures.
- Easy to dry by hanging upside down in small bunches in a cool, well-ventilated spot.
- Craspedia will make a cheerful addition to bright blue cornflowers or red tulips.

 Craspedia globosa

For Weddings:

More brides are including Craspedia in their wedding flowers as trends become more natural and unstructured. Its bright colour, texture and reliability have made it a popular flower for buttonhole bunches and country weddings where it will add a splash of vibrant colour and a sense of fun.

For Students:

Family: Asteraceae.

Genus: Craspedia.

Origin: Australia and New Zealand.

Flower Trivia: Craspedia grows in every area of Australia with the exception of the Northern Territory.

Crocosmia

Common Name: **Montbretia, Copper tips, Falling stars**

Availability: July–October.

Vase Life: Approx 7–10 days.

Flower Notes: Growing profusely in gardens and across the countryside, Crocosmia is a familiar sight in the early autumn with its arching flower stems and sword-like leaves. Medium stem length.

Colour Range: A fiery combination of orange, red and gold.

For the Florist:

- Ideal temperature range 8–10°C (46–50°F).
- Susceptible to ethylene gas.
- Avoid overcrowding in vases as stems can become tangled.
- Change water every 3–4 days, re-cutting stems each time and use flower food.
- Form: Line/Transitional.

For the Home:

- Re-cut stems and place in clean, fresh water with flower food.
- Remove lower flowers as they die, and change water every 3–4 days.
- An excellent cut flower both in water and floral foam.
- Arrange in a tall vase with gladioli and Chrysanthemum blooms.

For Weddings:

A lovely natural flower for autumn weddings in either tied posies or arrangements where its slim curved flower stem will provide an attractive contrast to fuller flowers such as roses and Dahlias. The seed heads are excellent for adding texture to wired work.

For Students:

Family: Iridaceae.

Genus: Crocosmia.

Origin: South Africa.

Flower Trivia: The name Crocosmia comes from the Greek 'krokos'- Saffron - and 'osme' - smell, referring to their saffron like scent when dried.

Crocosmia 'Amberglow'

Curcuma

Common Name: **Siam/Summer tulip**

Availability: April–October, peaks May–September.

Vase Life: Approx 7–14 days.

Flower Notes: An unusual shaped flower on a sturdy straight stem with delicately coloured bracts. It has a spicy, somewhat sweet scent. Medium stem length.

Colour Range: Pale pink/green, creamy white/green.

For the Florist:

- Ideal temperature range 12–20°C (54–68°F).
- Temperatures lower than 12°C (54°F) may damage the flower.
- A delicate flower, handle with care.
- Avoid storing in the dark, as this can cause the colour to fade.
- Sensitive to ethylene gas. Display in a warm spot with good air circulation.
- **Form:** Line.

For the Home:

- Re-cut stems and place in clean, fresh water.
- Display in a warm position in a brightly-lit spot, away from draughts.
- If arranging in floral foam, make sure the container is always topped up.
- For a striking, tropical display, arrange with Anthuriums and Moluccella.

For Weddings:

Not an easy flower to fit into the traditional wedding scheme, but a definite contender for something a little more funky and unusual. This flower would make a bold statement either as part of a structural design, or placed singly in a vase.

For Students:

Family: Zingiberaceae.

Genus: Curcuma.

Origin: South and South-east Asia.

Flower Trivia: In Thailand the Siam tulip or Krachiao flower as it is called locally, grows prolifically in the wild during the rainy season.

Curcuma alismatifolia

59

Cyclamen

Common Name: **Cyclamen, Persian Cyclamen, Sowbread**

Availability: October–February.

Vase Life: 10–14 days.

Flower Notes: Commercially cut Cyclamen is a relatively new product. Pretty with swept back petals and distinctive foliage, it is more commonly seen as a houseplant. Short stem length.

Colour Range: All shades of pink, red, white and bicoloured.

For the Florist:

- Ideal temperature range: 2–5°C (36–41°F).
- Make a vertical slit, 1cm (1/2") at the bottom of the stem to encourage the flower to take up water.
- Stand in clean, shallow water, flower food is not necessary.
- Store away from direct heat and draughts.
- **Form:** Round.

For the Home:

- Re-cut stems and display in a suitably sized vase.
- Despite their delicate appearance, Cyclamen have a good vase life.
- Their vase life will be shortened however if used in floral foam.
- Display in a simple bud vase, or with short stemmed flowers such as Muscari or snowdrops.

Cyclamen persicum

For Weddings:

Cyclamen are most appropriate in more delicate bridal work, they can be added into tied bridal posies, but may get overshadowed by larger, bolder flowers. Use in pink/white/pastel colour schemes or contrast the deeper shades of pink with burnt orange and lime. Their ivy-like leaves are lovely for wired work, the flowers can also be wired, but with care.

Flower meaning: Diffidence.

For Students:

Family: Primulaceae.

Genus: *Cyclamen persicum*.

Origin: Mediterranean, N. Africa.

Flower Trivia: *Cyclamen balearicum* (Balearic Cyclamen) is one of the very few Cyclamen to flower in only one colour, a fragrant, pure white.

Cymbidium

Common Name: **Cymbidium orchid, Boat orchid**

Availability: September–June.

Vase Life: Approx 14–21 days.

Flower Notes: A striking member of the orchid family with showy flowers of five petals surrounding a distinctively marked 'throat'. There are both large and mini varieties with up to 20 heads on a mini stem and 8–12 on a large.

Colour Range: White, lemon, yellow, gold, lime green, burgundy, pale pink, deep pink, red, peach.

For the Florist:

- Ideal temperature range 8–12°C (46–54°F).
- Translucent petals are a sign of exposure to low temperatures.
- If flowers begin to droop, mist to restore humidity.
- Sensitive to ethylene gas.
- Handle with care to avoid damaging the delicate 'throat' of the orchid.
- **Form:** Line/Round.

For the Home:

- Re-cut stems at an angle and place in clean, fresh water with flower food.
- Large stems can be top heavy, so a select a tall, sturdy vase.
- Flower food is recommended.
- Some Cymbidiums have a fragrant scent.

 Cymbidium 'Rosie'

For Weddings:

An almost faultless wedding flower for bridal bouquets or when used as the centrepiece of a sophisticated corsage. Whole stems of Cymbidium are imposing in large arrangements, and individual heads can be glued or wired into designs.

Flower meaning: Refinement.

For Students:

Family: Orchidaceae.

Genus: Cymbidium.

Origin: South East Asia.

Flower Trivia: : There are approximately 52 species of Cymbidium. They have been cultivated for thousands of years, and first came to Britain in the Victorian era.

Cynara

Common Name: **Globe artichoke, Cardoon**

Availability: February–November, peaks April–October.

Vase Life: Approx 7–10 days.

Flower Notes: An impressive sculptural flower similar to a giant thistle with a scaly green outer from which sprouts a fluffy crew-cut of a flower. Tall stem length.

Colour Range: Vivid purple, green.

For the Florist:

- Ideal temperature range 1–5°C (34–41°F).
- Re-cut stems and remove all foliage in contact with water.
- Use flower food to prevent leaves from yellowing and change water every 2–3 days.
- The flower will discolour before the outer lobes.
- **Form:** Round.

For the Home:

- Re-cut stems and place in clean, fresh water with flower food.
- Individual flowers will turn mouldy at the base after a few days although retain their colour on top.
- Unopened buds will flower over a period of time.
- Can be top heavy and spiky, handle with care and choose a vase that will hold their weight.

Cynara cardunculus

For Weddings:

For autumnal or winter weddings Cynara will add a touch of Victorian opulence to venue designs. Individual heads can be placed along tables for something a little more 'medieval'. Dried flower heads can be sprayed gold or silver for Christmas weddings.

For Students:

Family: Asteraceae.

Genus: Cynara.

Origin: Mediterranean, Northwest Africa and Canary Islands.

Flower Trivia: Popular in cuisine since Greek times, cardoons are used as vegetable rennet in cheese production.

Dahlia

Common Name: **Dahlia, Pinwheel**

Availability: July–November.

Vase Life: Approx 5–7 days.

Flower Notes: An old-fashioned garden flower which is currently enjoying something of a renaissance. Bold, bright and cheerful, it is a quintessential autumn flower. Sensitive to ethylene gas. Medium/tall stem length.

Colour Range: From deep burgundy to white and all colours in-between, with the exception of blue and green.

For the Florist:

- Ideal temperature range 2–8°C (36–46°F).
- Remove all foliage in contact with water and keep away from direct heat sources.
- Handle with care as the heads can shatter easily. Mist occasionally.
- Change water daily, re-cutting stems each time. Add flower food.
- **Stem Type:** Hollow.

For the Home:

- Re-cut stems and remove foliage in contact with water.
- Dahlias are water polluters, so change vase water daily.
- For maximum vase life, stand in a cool position and use flower food.
- The curled petals of Dahlias are attractive to insects, so shake the flower out gently just in case!
- Arrange in rustic style containers with Hypericum, Kniphofia or Amaranthus.

 Dahlia pinnata

For Weddings:

For a bride planning an autumn wedding and looking for seasonal, British-grown flowers, Dahlias should be high on the agenda. Add to tied posies with care, as the heads can be top heavy.

Flower meaning: Forever thine.

For Students:

Family: Asteraceae.

Genus: Dahlia.

Origin: Central America and Columbia.

Flower Trivia: The Aztecs originally cultivated Dahlias for food as well as for decorative purposes. It is the national flower of Mexico.

63

Daucus

Common Name: **Queen Anne's lace, Wild carrot, Bird's nest**

Availability: February–December.

Vase Life: Approx 10–14 days.

Flower Notes: Commonly found growing wild by the seashore and on waste land, the delicate flat flower head curls gently over its stalk as it matures, hence its common name, 'Bird's Nest'. Tall stem length.

Colour Range: Pinky red.

For the Florist:

- Ideal temperature range 2–5°C (36–41°F).
- Change water every 2–3 days, re-cutting stems each time and adding flower food.
- Remove all foliage in contact with water.
- Stems can easily tangle – hold the flowers upside down and gently pull apart to separate them.
- **Stem Type:** Hollow.
- **Form:** Round.

For the Home:

- Re-cut stems and place in clean, fresh water with flower food.
- Remove all foliage in contact with water and change water every 2–3 days, re-cutting stems each time.
- Keep out of direct heat, its flower life will be prolonged in cooler conditions.
- Arrange in a tall vase with natural garden flowers such as Delphinium and Phlox.

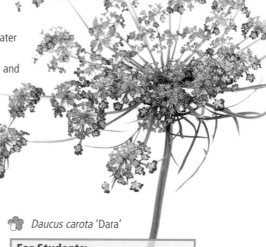

🌸 *Daucus carota* 'Dara'

For Weddings:

A pretty flower in an unusual shade of pink which would coordinate well with other summer flowers such as stocks, peonies and Salvia. Its wild, hedgerow look would be perfect for a bride looking for a natural, informal style.

For Students:

Family: Apiaceae.

Genus: Daucus.

Origin: Europe and South West Asia.

Flower Trivia: Known as Queen Anne's Lace due to its dark red centre, supposedly formed from a drop of blood from her pricked finger.

Delphinium

Common Name: **Lark's claw, Lark's heel**

Availability: April–November, peaks June–October.

Vase Life: Approx 7 days.

Flower Notes: A beautiful and stately cottage garden favourite and one of the few, true blue, tall flowers commonly available. Tall stem length.

Colour Range: All shades of blue, plus purple, lilac, pink and white.

For the Florist:

- Ideal temperature range 2–5°C (36–41°F).
- Frequent re-cutting of stems will help to prevent flower drop.
- Remove all foliage in contact with water which should be changed daily, re-cutting stems each time.
- Display away from direct heat sources.
- Very sensitive to ethylene gas.
- **Stem Type:** Hollow.
- **Form:** Line.

For the Home:

- Re-cut stems and place in clean, fresh water with flower food.
- Remove all foliage in contact with water, and change water daily, re-cutting stems each time.
- Display in a cool position, out of direct heat.
- All parts of the Delphinium are poisonous, so handle with care and wash hands after use.
- Arrange with sunflowers in a tall vase for a cheerful summery display.

 Delphinium 'Dewi Boy'

For Weddings:

A truly impressive flower, ideal for large showy arrangements and particularly suited for summer weddings. Smaller varieties such as 'Volkerfrieden' would complement their taller cousins when used in tied posies and shower bouquets.

Flower meaning: Big hearted.

For Students:

Family: Ranunculaceae.

Genus: Delphinium.

Origin: Native throughout the northern hemisphere.

Flower Trivia: Believed by the Greeks to have magical properties, Delphinium was reportedly used in Transylvania to ward witches away from stables.

Dendrobium

Common Name: **Singapore orchid**

Availability: All year round.

Vase Life: Approx 14–21 days.

Flower Notes: A very pretty and popular orchid with arching sprays of small, delicate star-shaped flowers with a waxy appearance. Short stem length.

Colour Range: Pure white, cerise pink, purple, lime, some with contrasting throats.

For the Florist:

- Minimum storage temperature 15°C (59°F).
- Remove all packaging on arrival, re-cut stems and stand in shallow water.
- Handle with care as the petals crease easily and don't let flowers touch the water.
- Keep away from draughts and direct heat sources. Misting occasionally will help to prolong vase life.
- **Form:** Line/Transitional.

For the Home:

- Re-cut stems and stand in shallow water.
- Make sure flower heads are not in contact with water.
- However, if flowers are limp, submerging them briefly in warm water will revive them.
- Display away from draughts and cool spots.

 Dendrobium 'Living Dreams White'

For Weddings:

Very popular in shower bouquets because of its elegant trailing habit, Singapore orchids are also ideal for wired work, especially in corsages as the flowers and buds are extremely light. Individual flower heads can also be used for hair pieces and for decorating cakes.

For Students:

Family: Orchidaceae.

Genus: Dendrobium.

Origin: Tropical Asia, Australia.

Flower Trivia: There are over a thousand known species of Dendrobium; commercial varieties are exported mainly from Thailand, Singapore and Hawaii. The name means 'like a butterfly'.

Dianthus barbatus

Common Name: **Sweet william**

Availability: April–June.

Vase Life: Approx 5–10 days.

Flower Notes: An old-fashioned cottage garden favourite, sweet-scented with pretty fringed petals, its fragrance reminiscent of summers past. Short/medium stem length.

Colour Range: A cheerful mix of purple, pink, burgundy, lilac and white.

 Dianthus barbatus

For the Florist:

- Ideal temperature range 2–5°C (36–41°F).
- Remove all foliage in contact with water which should be changed daily, re-cutting stems between the nodes each time.
- Ensure all vases and containers are clean, and use flower food.
- Curved stems will not straighten after the flower has been cut.
- Sensitive to ethylene gas, so needs good air circulation.

For the Home:

- Rinse stems if necessary and re-cut, placing them in clean, fresh water.
- Remove all foliage below the water line and change water every day, re-cutting stems each time.
- Keep out of direct heat sources to prolong vase life, flower food is recommended.
- Cut stems between the nodes for maximum water uptake.
- Achieve a natural country look by arranging Sweet Williams with *Alchemilla mollis* and Astrantia.

Dianthus barbatus
Green Trick

For Weddings:

Given the Royal seal of approval when included in the wedding bouquet of the Duchess of Cambridge in 2011, scented sweet william is perfect for a bride looking for a natural style and who is also keen to use seasonally grown flowers. The moss-like, textured variety Green Trick will add further contrast to bridal tied designs and arrangements.

Flower meaning: Gallantry.

For Students:

Family: Caryophyllaceae.

Genus: Dianthus.

Origin: Mountains of Southern Europe & N/E Asia.

Flower Trivia: Sweet william flowers are edible, with a peppery, clove-like flavour. Add into summer salads and cocktails.

Dianthus (Spray)

Common Name: **Spray carnation, Mini carnation**

Availability: All year round.

Vase Life: Approx 14–21 days.

Flower Notes: A long-standing favourite with a fantastic vase life and available in a huge spectrum of colours. Virtually indispensable in traditional arrangements and bouquets. Medium stem length.

Colour Range: From white to deep purple and all colours in-between with the exception of blue.

 Dianthus caryophyllus nana 'Rhodos'

For the Florist:

- Ideal temperature range 4–8°C (39–46°F).
- Remove all foliage in contact with water and add flower food.
- Very sensitive to ethylene gas, so ensure flowers have good air circulation at all times.
- Change water every 3–4 days, re-cutting stems each time.
- **Form:** Transitional.

For the Home:

- Re-cut stems between nodes and place in clean, fresh water.
- Wilting and browning of flowers is a sign of exposure to ethylene gas.
- Stems can become slimy if stood in deep water so display in shallow water which should be changed every 3–4 days, re-cutting stems each time.
- Arrange with similar sized summer flowers for a natural look such as Nigella, spray roses or Veronica.

 Dianthus plumarius

For Weddings:

A pretty flower which is equally versatile in vase designs or arranged in floral foam. The more delicate shades would complement most colour schemes and their dainty green buds are great for adding texture in wired work. The scented *Dianthus plumarius* (pinks) are a perfect vintage wedding flower.

For Students:

Family: Caryophyllaceae.

Genus: Dianthus.

Origin: Native to Southern Europe and Asia.

Flower Trivia: With over 300 species in the genus and cultivated for over 2,000 years, carnations are one of the world's most popular cut flowers.

Dianthus (Standard)

Common Name: **Carnation, Sims**

Availability: All year round.

Vase Life: Approx 14–21 days.

Flower Notes: A universally known flower, undeservedly seen by some as 'old-fashioned'. Their sheer range of colours and superb lasting qualities should really make them the nation's favourite. Medium stem length.

Colour Range: All colours in all tones, shades and tints apart from blue and black.

For the Florist:

- Ideal temperature range 4–8°C (39–46°F).
- Remove all foliage in contact with water and change water every 2–3 days.
- Handle with care as stems can snap easily.
- Always cut stems between the nodes to aid water take up.
- Very sensitive to ethylene gas, so display in a spot with good air circulation.
- **Form:** Round.

For the Home:

- Re-cut stems between the nodes and place in clean, fresh water with flower food.
- Remove all foliage below the water line and change water every 2–3 days.
- Tease out closed carnations by cupping the flower between thumb and forefinger and fluffing gently.
- Carnations work well with bold flowers; try large-headed roses, sunflowers or lilies.

 Dianthus 'Prado Pino'

For Weddings:
The trend for retro styling has given the humble carnation something of a resurgence in popularity and new varieties in delicate, antique shades are transforming their look. Carnations are good value for money, reliable and more versatile in design work than many give them credit for.
Flower meaning: Devotion.

For Students:
Family: Caryophyllaceae.
Genus: Dianthus.
Origin: Native to Southern Europe and Asia.
Flower Trivia: One of the world's best selling flowers; the carnation is the national flower of Spain, and the state flower of Ohio.

Digitalis

Common Name: **Foxglove, Witches' gloves, Fairy thimbles**

Availability: June and July.

Vase Life: Approx 7–10 days.

Flower Notes: More commonly recognised as a wild flower, the tall spikes of foxgloves are synonymous with summer and old-fashioned cottage gardens. Tall stem length.

Colour Range: Rich purple/pink.

For the Florist:

- Ideal temperature range 1–2°C (34–36°F).
- Change water every other day, re-cutting stems each time and add flower food.
- Keep away from direct heat and draughts.
- Sensitive to ethylene gas, so display in a spot with good air circulation.
- Wash hands and clean workbench after use.
- **Stem Type:** Hollow.
- **Form:** Line.

For the Home:

- Re-cut stems and place in clean, fresh water with flower food.
- Wilted flowers are a source of ethylene gas, so remove them as they fade.
- Re-cut stems and change the water every other day.
- A poisonous plant, always wash hands after use.

Digitalis purpurea

For Weddings:

A fantastic flower for large impressive pedestal designs or simply massed together in large vases. It would be a very individual choice of flower for a bride looking for a natural, rural style. Not recommended for wiring work.

Flower Meaning: Stateliness.

For Students:

Family: Plantaginaceae.

Genus: Digitalis.

Origin: Europe, Asia and N/W Africa.

Flower Trivia: Digitalis means 'finger like' as the tubular flowers fit snugly over human finger tips.

Echinacea

Common Name: **Purple/American coneflower**

Availability: June–December, peaks June–October.

Vase Life: Approx 7–10 days.

Flower Notes: Pronounced 'Eck-IN-nay-cher'. A summer flowering perennial with a large, showy flower head, long slender petals and a spiky cone-shaped centre. Medium stem length.

Colour Range: Pinky/purple with a burnt orange centre.

For the Florist:

- Ideal temperature range 5–10°C (41–50°F).
- Keep away from direct heat sources and draughts.
- Can be used in design work with or without petals.
- Remove any foliage in contact with water and add flower food.
- **Form:** Round.

For the Home:

- Re-cut stems and place in clean, fresh water.
- Remove petals as they fade, the solid centre will last up to three weeks without them.
- Flower food is recommended, and vase water should be changed every 2–3 days.
- To dry, hang upside down in small bunches tied with elastic bands, in a cool, airy place.
- For a cottage garden look arrange with roses, Veronica or scabious.

 Echinacea purpurea

For Weddings:

Echinacea would be an interesting choice for a wedding flower with its combination of pink petals and orange centre. It would fit in well with a seasonal, autumnal colour scheme. Can be used either in floral foam or water. Use the centre of the flower to add texture to wired work.

For Students:

Family: Asteraceae.

Genus: Echinacea.

Origin: USA.

Flower Trivia: A popular herbal remedy, Echinacea is believed to be a deterrent against colds and flu. Native Americans used the root as a treatment for snake bites and rabies.

Echinops

Common Name: **Globe thistle**

Availability: May–October.

Vase Life: Approx 14–21 days.

Flower Notes: A perfect ball-shaped head of tiny star-shaped flowers with a spiky appearance. Its spiny, thistle-like foliage has a metallic blue sheen. Medium stem length.

Colour Range: Silvery blue, purple.

For the Florist:

- Ideal temperature range 2–5°C (36–41°F).
- Re-cut stems and remove all foliage in contact with water.
- Change water every 4–5 days, re-cutting stems each time.
- Prefers cooler conditions out of direct sun and heat sources.
- **Form:** Round.

For the Home:

- Re-cut stems and place in clean, fresh water which should be changed every 4–5 days.
- The foliage will not last as long as the flowers, remove any that start to turn yellow and wilt.
- Flower food is recommended to keep the flower's lustrous shine.
- Easy to dry - remove all foliage and hang upside down in a cool spot with good air circulation.
- For a touch of vintage style, arrange with spray roses and scented pinks.

 Echinops ritro 'Veitch's Blue'

For Weddings:

Wonderful for adding texture to designs and wired work, Echinops lasts well in floral foam and will coordinate with most summer and autumn colour schemes. Arrange with softer flowers like Eustoma or scabious to make the most of its spiky appearance. Both leaves and flower heads are prickly, so take care if using in tied designs.

For Students:

Family: Asteraceae.

Genus: Echinops.

Origin: South Eastern Europe.

Flower Trivia: Just as prickly as the globe thistle is *Echinops telfairi* except that it is not a flower, but a mammal-like hedgehog, the only one in its genus, and endemic to Madagascar.

Eremurus

Common Name: **Foxtail lily, Desert candle, King's spear**

Availability: April–September, peaks June–August.

Vase Life: Approx 7 days.

Flower Notes: Pronounced 'E-re-MUIR-us'. A native desert flower, capable of growing over three metres in height. Its tall, slender spires are covered with hundreds of tiny star-shaped flowers. Tall stem length.

Colour Range: Yellow, copper, salmon, orange.

For the Florist:

- Ideal temperature range 8–10°C (46–50°F).
- Don't store in a cooler or refrigerate as low temperatures shorten vase life.
- Curved stems will not straighten once cut.
- Remove flowers as they die as they emit ethylene gas.
- Change water every 2–3 days, re-cutting stems each time.
- **Form:** Line.

For the Home:

- Re-cut stems and place in clean, fresh water with flower food.
- Eremurus blooms from the bottom up. Remove wilted flowers to improve appearance.
- Vase water should be changed every 2–3 days, re-cutting the stems each time.
- Due to their height, they need a sturdy, tall vase; try arranging them with Anthuriums or Strelitzia for a colourful display.

For Weddings:

A flower for the modern bride, perhaps one with a tropical theme as these flowers work very well with bold, bright colours and shapes. They would not look out of place though in more traditional designs, and are excellent for adding height and volume to venue arrangements.
Flower meaning: Endurance.

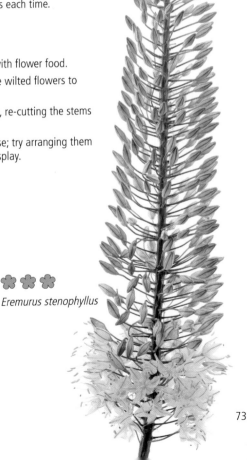

Eremurus stenophyllus

For Students:

Family: Asphodelaceae.
Genus: Eremurus.
Origin: Iran, Turkey and Afghanistan.
Flower Trivia: Its name comes from the Greek for 'desert' and 'tail', a reference to both its shape and origins.

Eryngium

Common Name: **Sea holly**

Availability: All year round.

Vase Life: Approx 10–14 days.

Flower Notes: Pronounced 'E-RIN-gee-um'. Often mistaken for a thistle, Eryngium is a popular garden plant with attractive blue/grey foliage. As a wild flower it can be found growing on sand dunes and shingle banks. Medium stem length.

Colour Range: Silvery blue, blue/grey, bright blue, purple.

For the Florist:

- Ideal temperature range 8–10°C (46–50°F).
- Less mature stems will absorb more water, so check vase levels regularly.
- Remove all foliage in contact with water which should be changed every 3-4 days.
- Unopened flowers will not develop further.
- **Stem Type:** Hollow.
- **Form:** Transitional.

Eryngium 'Orion'

For the Home:

- Re-cut stems and place in clean, fresh water.
- Remove all foliage in contact with water and add flower food.
- They are thirsty flowers, so check vase levels and change water every 3–4 days.
- Remove any yellowing foliage to improve the flower's appearance.
- Contrast with rich reds and oranges, try Gerberas, roses or Chrysanthemums.

For Weddings:

A useful substitute for thistle in weddings with a Scottish theme, Eryngium makes great buttonholes and looks good with a kilt! Use it to give depth and texture to deep red and cream colour schemes or rich autumnal golds and oranges. Might be a little too prickly for hand-tied posies or wrist corsages.

For Students:

Family: Apiaceae.

Genus: Eryngium.

Origin: Central Europe and Siberia.

Flower Trivia: The thick fleshy roots were once peeled and boiled with sugar to make candied eryngoes, a sweet which was believed to have restorative properties.

Eucharis

Availability: All year round, more limited in summer.

Vase Life: Approx 7–10 days.

Flower Notes: An elegant flower, daffodil-like in appearance, bearing three to six nodding heads on a slim leafless stem. Medium stem length.

Colour Range: Pure white with a yellow centre.

For the Florist:

- Ideal temperature range 5–10°C (41–50°F).
- Lower temperatures can inhibit flower development and cause the petals to discolour.
- Mist and cover with plastic to restore humidity if flowers begin to droop.
- Handle with care, as the flowers bruise easily.
- Buds will continue to open after the flower has been cut.
- **Form:** Round.

For the Home:

- Re-cut stems every 3–4 days.
- Removing older flowers will encourage buds to open.
- To avoid the flower drying out, mist occasionally and keep vases and floral foam topped up with water.
- Keep out of cold spots, Eucharis prefer warmer temperatures.

Eucharis x grandiflora

For Weddings:

Use the dainty and elegant Eucharis in venue and church arrangements when more limited designs are required which will really show off their delicate beauty. Suitable for wiring, although handle carefully as they can bruise easily. They will give an air of sophistication to bridal bouquets and tied posies.

For Students:

Family: Amaryllidaceae.

Genus: Eucharis.

Origin: Central and South America.

Flower Trivia: First named as a species in 1854, its name comes from the Greek 'eu' meaning 'good, true' and 'charis' 'loveliness'.

Eupatorium

Common Name: **White snakeroot, Indian sanicle**

Availability: January–November, peaks July–September.
Vase Life: Approx 10–14 days.
Flower Notes: A perennial wild flower which grows on rocky soil and woodland. It has clusters of tiny fluffy flowers on sturdy stems with heart-shaped leaves. Tall stem length.
Colour Range: White, pinky red.

For the Florist:

- Ideal temperature range 5–8°C (41–46°F).
- Remove any foliage in contact with water and add flower food.
- Change water every 4–5 days re-cutting stems each time.
- Display out of direct heat sources.
- Can be a skin irritant, so wash hands after use.
- **Form:** Round.

For the Home:

- Re-cut stems at an angle and place in clean, fresh water.
- Change water every 4–5 days, re-cutting stems each time and add flower food.
- A poisonous flower, so display away from young children and pets.
- Use Eupatorium to fill out vases of roses, Gerberas or sunflowers.

 Eupatorium rugosum 'Braunlaub'

For Weddings:

A sturdy, reliable flower, which although not significant enough for bridal flowers would be very useful for filling out large reception/church arrangements. Its colouring and style would suit a summer or early autumn wedding. Not recommended in hand-tied posies or in wired work as it can have an irritant effect on some people.

For Students:

Family: Asteraceae.
Genus: Eupatorium.
Origin: North America.
Flower Trivia: Native Americans used the plants as a treatment for snake bites, as well as a host of other complaints. *Eupatorium rugosum* is synonymous with *Ageratum altissima*.

Euphorbia

Common Name: **Scarlet plume**

Availability: Peaks October–December with limited availability the rest of the year.

Vase Life: Approx 6–8 days.

Flower Notes: A true winter flower with slim arching stems covered with tiny, brightly coloured flowers and slim oval leaves. Tall stem length.

Colour Range: Creamy white, orange, yellow, gold, red.

For the Florist:

- Ideal temperature range 8–12°C (46–54°F).
- Sensitive to temperature fluctuations and ethylene gas.
- Removing the leaves will improve its appearance for design work.
- The latex produced from the stem is an irritant, gloves are recommended for cutting and conditioning.
- **Stem Type:** Latex producing.
- **Form:** Line.

For the Home:

- Re-cut stems at an angle, preferably underwater as this limits latex seepage, and add flower food.
- If flowers become limp, re-cut stems and stand in hot water to revive them.
- Latex that congeals on the skin can be removed by soap and water.
- A poisonous flower, so not recommended in houses with small children or pets.

 Euphorbia fulgens 'Quicksilver'

For Weddings:

The rich colours of Euphorbia make them ideal for a winter or late autumn wedding where their arched stems will add elegance to church and venue arrangements. Its sap can be an irritant, so not recommended for bridal flowers or wired work.

Flower meaning: Persistence.

For Students:

Family: Euphorbiaceae.
Genus: Euphorbia.
Origin: Mexico.
Flower Trivia: One of the most diverse plant groups in the world, Euphorbia was named in honour of Euphorbus, a Greek physician who supposedly used its resin as a herbal remedy.

Eustoma

Common Name: **Lisianthus, Prairie gentian, Texas bluebell**

Availability: All year round.

Vase Life: Approx 12–16 days.

Flower Notes: An extremely popular cut flower with grey-green foliage that grows in both single and double forms. The flowers are extremely pretty, similar in style to a rose. Medium stem length.

Colour Range: Pure white, cream, pale lime, rose pink, cerise pink, lilac, deep purple. Also bicoloured.

For the Florist:

- Ideal temperature range 8–15°C (46–59°F).
- Flowers can be harmed by cold storage under 8° (46°F).
- Warm temperatures will encourage flowers to open.
- Re-cut stems every 3–4 days to keep a steady flow of water to the flower head, changing the water at the same time.
- **Stem Type:** Soft.
- **Form:** Transitional/Line.

For the Home:

- Re-cut stems at an angle and place in clean, fresh water with flower food.
- Remove any leaves in contact with water.
- Furled buds will continue to 'unwind' after the flower has been cut.
- Re-cut stems and change water every 3–4 days.
- Make the most of Eustoma's summery prettiness by arranging them with scabious, Nigella or Freesia.

 Eustoma russellianum 'Picot Pink'

For Weddings:

Its range of soft colours and delicate appearance make Eustoma a very versatile and extremely useful wedding flower. The slightly arching stems and rose-like blooms look wonderful in tied or shower bouquets and it can also be used in wired work, although with care, as the soft stems can snap easily.

For Students:

Family: Gentianaceae.

Genus: Eustoma.

Origin: Southern USA.

Flower Trivia: Eustoma is a native American wildflower. It can be seen growing on the prairies of Colorado, and as far south as Texas.

Forsythia

Common Name: **Golden bell**

Availability: November–April, peaks January–March.

Vase Life: Approx 5–8 days.

Flower Notes: The star-shaped flowers of Forsythia are produced before the leaves on this informal bushy shrub which brightens up many gardens in early spring. Tall stem length.

Colour Range: Bright yellow.

For the Florist:

- Ideal temperature range 4–5°C (39–41°F).
- Use specialised shrub food if available to encourage the flowers to open.
- Remove side branches below and just above the water line to prevent the stems becoming tangled.
- Change water every 2–3 days re-cutting stems each time.
- **Stem Type:** Woody.
- **Form:** Line.

For the Home:

- Re-cut stems with secateurs and stand in clean, fresh water.
- Add flower food and change water every 2–3 days, re-cutting stems each time.
- Stand in a cool spot out of direct heat sources with good air circulation.
- Arrange full length stems of Forsythia in tall vases for a welcome breath of spring indoors.

 Forsythia x intermedia 'Spectabilis'

For Weddings:

One of the few tall spring flowers, Forsythia is indispensable for large impressive arrangements in churches and venues – as long as the colour scheme fits! Great for adding stature and height to reception table designs.
Flower meaning: Anticipation.

For Students:

Family: Oleaceae.
Genus: Forsythia.
Origin: Eastern Asia.
Flower Trivia: Named in honour of the Scottish horticulturalist William Forsyth, one of the founders of the Royal Horticultural Society.

79

Freesia

Common Name: **Freesia**

Availability: All year round.

Vase Life: Approx 5–7 days.

Flower Notes: A popular, highly fragrant flower with delicate arched stems. Although traditionally a spring flower, modern production has enabled quality Freesia to be available for twelve months of the year. Short stem length.

Colour Range: Pure white, lemon, yellow, orange, gold, amber, pale pink, deep pink, lilac, purple.

For the Florist:

- Ideal temperature range 5–8°C (41–46°F).
- Cooler temperatures can reduce its fragrance.
- Give time for flowers to absorb water fully before using in design work.
- Sensitive to ethylene gas.
- **Stem Type:** Soft.
- **Form:** Line/Transitional.

For the Home:

- Re-cut stems and place in clean, fresh water with flower food.
- Stems can get easily tangled, so handle with care.
- Remove wilted heads to encourage further flowering.
- Display with Genista or hyacinths for a scented, spring pick-me-up.

 Freesia 'Grace'

For Weddings:

A very versatile wedding flower, which although delicate in appearance is strong enough to use in arrangements and shower bouquets. Freesias' curved stems will add a lovely line to tied posies and they can be added into wired work, although they will dehydrate quickly in hot weather.

Flower meaning: Innocence and trust.

For Students:

Family: Iridaceae.

Genus: Freesia.

Origin: South Africa.

Flower Trivia: Named after the German physician Friedrich Freese, Freesia is one of the world's most popular cut flowers. There are some people who unfortunately cannot detect the sweet scent of Freesias.

Fritillaria

Common Name: Chequered Lily, Snake's Head Fritillary, Guinea flower

Availability: February–May.

Vase Life: Approx 7–10 days.

Flower Notes: A spring flowering bulb with a delicate, nodding head. Once a common wild flower, modern farming techniques have almost wiped out the population and it is now an endangered species. Short stem length.

Colour Range: Maroon with chocolate brown markings.

For the Florist:

- Ideal temperature range 2–5°C (36–41°F).
- Cut away any white parts of the stem, as they will not take up water.
- Store in a cool place away from sources of ethylene gas.
- Stand in deep water when first conditioning, adding specialised bulb food if available.

For the Home:

- Re-cut stems and stand in clean, fresh, deep water.
- Flower food is recommended, change water every 2/3 days.
- Stand in a cool spot out of draughts and direct heat.
- Some Fritillaria can have a somewhat strong, not very pleasant odour.
- Arrange with late flowering hellebores, Muscari or tulips.

 Fritillaria meleagris

For Weddings:

Although a firm favourite with some floral designers this would be an unusual flower to choose for a wedding as it doesn't take well to floral foam and has a scent which some people dislike. For a spring wedding, display it in simple vases with similarly sized spring flowers, such as tulips and Ranunculus. A little too delicate for tied poises or wired work.

For Students:

Family: Liliaceae.

Genus: Fritillaria.

Origin: Middle East.

Flower Trivia: One of the most famous Fritillaria meadows is at Magdalen College, Oxford where they have been growing since 1785.

Fritillaria

Common Name: **Persian lily**

Availability: April–May.

Vase Life: Approx 7–10 days.

Flower Notes: An impressive spring flowering bulb, with tall spires of showy, conical bell shaped flowers with up to 30 on each stem. Medium/tall stem length.

Colour Range: Pale green, maroon and plum.

For the Florist:

- Ideal temperature range 2–5°C (36–41°F).
- Cut away any white parts of the stem as they will not take up water.
- Re-cut stems frequently to keep a flow of water to the flower head.
- Condition well before use and use specialised bulb food if available.
- A fragile flower, handle with care.

For the Home:

- Re-cut stems and stand in clean, fresh water.
- Change water every 2–3 days, recutting stems and adding flower food.
- Stand in a cool spot out of draughts and direct heat.
- Some Fritillaria can have a somewhat strong, not very pleasant odour.
- This unusual tall spring flower will work well arranged with Forsythia or Hippeastrum.

 Fritillaria persica 'Ivory Bells'

For Weddings:

Not a flower for intricate bridal work, but lovely in arrangements, particularly more limited designs where its form and flowers can be appreciated. Can be used in either floral foam or in vase designs and would be perfect for a spring wedding. Poisonous, so handle with care and wash hands after use. Not recommended for wired work.

For Students:

Family: Liliaceae.

Genus: Fritillaria.

Origin: Middle East.

Flower Trivia: Janis Ruksans, an avid Latvian plant collector and nursery man is largely credited for developing and preserving *Fritillaria persica*.

Galanthus

Common Name: **Snowdrop**

Availability: January–March.

Vase Life: Approx 4–5 days.

Flower Notes: A winter flowering perennial, one of the first flowering bulbs of the season. Threatened in their natural habitat, it is now illegal to collect bulbs from the wild. Short stem length.

Colour Range: Pure white with green markings.

For the Florist:

- Ideal temperature range 1–4°C (34–39°F).
- Cut a small amount from the bottom of the stem using scissors.
- Store in a cool place away from sources of ethylene gas.
- Stand in deep water when first conditioning, adding specialised bulb food if available.
- Using plants is the most practical way to obtain snowdrops in season.

For the Home:

- Re-cut stems with scissors and stand in clean, fresh water.
- Change water daily adding a small amount of flower food.
- Stand in a cool spot out of draughts and direct heat.
- Arrange in a small vase or jug with ivy and berries for a petite seasonal display!

Galanthus nivalis

For Weddings:

Snowdrops don't often make it onto brides' wish lists, as they are regarded largely as a garden flower. However, for a winter bride who is keen on keeping it seasonal they would be a delightful addition to bridal reception flowers when arranged in simple jars or jugs. Too small for only the daintiest of tied posies, they are too delicate for wired work.

Flower Meaning: Hope.

For Students:

Family: Amaryllidaceae.

Genus: Galanthus.

Origin: Europe & Middle East.

Flower Trivia: Primrose Warburg, wife of botanist E. F. Warburg, has a snowdrop named after her. It has distinctive yellow markings.

Genista

Common Name: **Bridal veil broom**

Availability: January–April.

Vase Life: Approx 5–8 days.

Flower Notes: This elegant, sweet-scented shrub has long slender, leafless branches covered with tiny, pea-shaped flowers. Medium stem length.

Colour Range: Creamy white, lemon; often dyed other colours such as orange or blue.

For the Florist:

- Ideal temperature range 1–2°C (34–36°F) with a maximum of no more than 5°C (41°F).
- Sensitive to ethylene gas which will shorten the vase life of the flower.
- Good air circulation is needed to prevent botrytis which can result in flower drop.
- Change water and re-cut stems every 2–3 days.
- **Form:** Line.

For the Home:

- Re-cut stems and place in fresh, shallow water with flower food.
- Make sure that no flowers are submerged as this can introduce bacteria into the water.
- Keep in a cool spot, as excessive heat will cause early flower drop.
- Use Genista to add a delicate outline to chunkier spring flowers such as tulips or daffodils.

 Genista monosperma
(Syn. Retama monosperma)

For Weddings:

The slim, arching branches of Genista are perfect for adding line to spring tieds and vase designs. They are so light that they will sway gently when carried, giving a subtle hint of movement. Very flexible, Genista can be looped or wound into designs and is very effective in wired work.

For Students:

Family: Papilionaceae.

Genus: Genista.

Origin: Mediterranean, North Africa.

Flower Trivia: *'Planta genista'* was the emblem of Geoffrey of Anjou, father of Henry II, the first Plantagenet king, who reportedly wore a sprig of common broom in his hat.

Gentiana

Availability: January–March, July–October.

Vase Life: Approx 14–21 days.

Flower Notes: Gentian is one of the few true blue flowers; the alpine variety is very popular with gardeners for growing in rock gardens and stone troughs. Medium stem length.

Colour Range: Ultramarine, white.

For the Florist:

- Ideal temperature range 2–5°C (36–41°F).
- Remove all foliage below water level.
- Re-cut stems and change water in vases every 3–4 days.
- Closed buds will not continue to open after the flower has been cut.
- Form: Line.

For the Home:

- Re-cut stems at an angle and place in clean, fresh water.
- A long-lasting flower, so change vase water and re-cut stems every 3–4 days.
- Keep in a cool spot, away from excessive heat.
- Arrange in a tall vase with either pink lilies, Alstroemeria or sunflowers.

 Gentiana 'Ashiro-No-Aki'

For Weddings:

The stems of Gentian are too stiff for informal wedding designs, but it's extremely reliable for using in large church or reception/venue arrangements. Its brilliant blue colour will contrast strikingly with rich autumnal colour schemes and individual flower heads can be used in wired work.

Flower meaning: Sweet be thy dreams.

For Students:

Family: Gentianaceae.

Genus: Gentiana.

Origin: The cut flower varieties originate from Japan.

Flower Trivia: Gentian is popular in herbal medicine and as a flavouring. The Italian brewery Birra Del Borgo has produced a spiced ale 'Genziana' based on the roots of the Gentian flower.

Gerbera

Common Name: **Transvaal/Barberton daisy**

Availability: All year round.

Vase Life: Approx 5–10 days.

Flower Notes: Pronounced 'Jer-ber-ra'. Its simple daisy shape and bold colours have made the Gerbera a modern day flower classic. Available in both large headed and mini forms. Medium stem length.

Colour Range: A full spectrum of colours with the exception of blue, black and green.

For the Florist:

- Ideal temperature range 5–8°C (41–46°F).
- Re-cut stem ends on arrival, removing any heels as they will not take up water.
- Heads will need supporting as the flower drinks, suspend in perforated cardboard or chicken wire over a tall bucket.
- Stand Gerberas for at least four hours in deep water before using in design work.
- Once conditioned, display in shallow water as the hairs on the stems will draw water upwards, which can cause stem rot.
- **Stem Type:** Hollow/Hairy.
- **Form:** Round.

For the Home:

- Re-cut stems at an angle and place in clean, fresh, shallow water.
- Use flower food as Gerberas are very sensitive to bacteria. Make sure all vases and containers are clean.
- Keep out of direct heat sources, they prefer cooler conditions.
- Gerberas will last longer in vases than when arranged in floral foam.

 Gerbera 'Explorer'

For Weddings:

The trendy, colourful Gerbera is an extremely popular wedding flower. Perfect for a more informal style of ceremony, whether carried as a cheerful tied posy or arranged individually in vases. They make a striking focal flower in large designs and can be used for buttonholes, but handle with care.

For Students:

Family: Asteraceae.

Genus: Gerbera.

Origin: South Africa.

Flower Trivia: Although Gerbera appears to be a thoroughly modern flower it was first named in 1737 after Traugott Gerber, a German doctor and keen botanist.

Gladiolus

Common Name: **Sword/Spear lily, Gladdie, Corn flag**

Availability: May–November, peaking July–October.

Vase Life: Approx 10–14 days.

Flower Notes: Characterised by large funnel-shaped flowers on tall, slim stems, gladioli are a late summer/early autumn classic. Generally tall stem length, although the 'Nanus' varieties are much shorter.

Colour Range: A wide range of colours including lime green – no blue however.

For the Florist:

- Ideal temperature range 2–8°C (36–46°F).
- Cut up to 10cm (5") from the bottom of the stems before standing in deep, cool water.
- Always store upright, as gladioli will grow naturally towards the light.
- Display in a cool place, away from sources of ethylene gas.
- Re-cut stems, replacing water every 2–3 days; add flower food.
- Form: Line.

For the Home:

- Re-cut stems at an angle and place in clean, fresh water with flower food.
- To ensure full flowering, change water and re-cut stems every 2–3 days.
- Nipping out the top of the flower spike will encourage the stems to stay upright.
- Gladioli look fantastic arranged on their own in a tall vase. Add lilies or sunflowers for extra drama.

 Gladiolus 'Lemon Drop'

For Weddings:

The tall stems of gladioli are indispensable when it comes to large pedestal arrangements, indeed for any designs that need height and impact. The smaller varieties, sometimes called 'bridal' or 'painted ladies' can be used in shower bouquets and also in wired work. **Flower meaning:** Generosity.

For Students:

Family: Iridaceae.

Genus: Gladiolus.

Origin: South Africa.

Flower Trivia: It has been said that the indefatigable Dame Edna Everage is almost single handedly responsible for reviving the popularity of 'gladdies' in Australia.

Gloriosa

Common Name: **Glory/Flame lily**

Availability: All year round.

Vase Life: Approx 10–14 days on the vine, 4–5 days as individual blooms.

Flower Notes: A spectacular climbing plant with vibrant curled-back petals. Available as either individual blooms in air-filled bags or as longer lengths of cut vine.

Colour Range: Fiery red, yellow and rich pink with yellow/lime margins.

For the Florist:

- Ideal temperature range 6–10°C (43–50°F). Lower temperatures will cause the flowers to discolour.
- If vacuumed-packed, flowers can be left in the packaging for up to five days.
- Once bags are opened re-cut stems and place in fresh water with flower food, misting occasionally.
- Handle with care, cutting, rather than pulling the delicate tendrils to separate stems.
- Toxic, wash hands and clean work benches thoroughly after handling.
- **Stem Type:** Soft.
- **Form:** Round.

For the Home:

- Re-cut stems at an angle and place in clean, fresh water with flower food.
- Revive limp flowers by submerging in warm water for a few minutes.
- Keep out of sunlight and direct heat sources and mist gently every other day.
- Arrange Gloriosa in a low bowl with orange roses and lime Chrysanthemum.

 Gloriosa superba 'Rothschildiana'

For Weddings:

These amazing flowers would be the stars of any wedding with a tropical, colourful theme. They would look superb tumbling out of a shower bouquet, particularly if teamed with orchids and Anthuriums. Can be used as a buttonhole or part of a corsage.

For Students:

Family: Colchicaceae.

Genus: Gloriosa.

Origin: Tropical Africa.

Flower Trivia: All parts of Gloriosa contain colchicine, a natural toxic which was once used to treat gout and other rheumatic complaints.

Gomphocarpus

Common Name: **Balloon cotton bush**

Availability: All year round.

Vase Life: Approx 7–10 days.

Flower Notes: Pronounced 'Gom-fo-car-pus'. This perennial shrub has papery, bladder-shaped fruits borne in the autumn which are covered with soft, bristle-like hairs. Medium stem length.

Colour Range: Pale green.

For the Florist:

- Ideal temperature range 2–4°C (36–39°F).
- Remove any leaves in contact with water which should be changed every 3–4 days.
- It exudes a milky sap when cut, rinse stem ends thoroughly under a running tap before using.
- The seed pods are quite delicate and can damage easily, handle with care.
- **Stem Type:** Latex producing.
- **Form:** Round.

For the Home:

- Re-cut stems and stand in clean, fresh water.
- Flower food is recommended, and water should be changed every 2–3 days.
- Rinse the stem ends to remove excess sap and always wash hands after use.
- Use Gomphocarpus as a foil to enhance bolder flowers such as Dahlias or sunflowers.

 Gomphocarpus fruticosus 'Moby Dick'
(Syn. *Asclepias fruticosa*)

For Weddings:

Use this unusual 'flower' in showy reception and venue designs where it will coordinate well with whites and yellows and add texture to rich autumn colours. Individual fruits can be floated in water in goldfish bowls for a table centre that will be a guaranteed talking point amongst guests!

For Students:

Family: Asclepiadaceae.

Genus: Gomphocarpus.

Origin: South Africa.

Flower Trivia: Although poisonous to livestock, the leaves of Gomphocarpus were used in herbal medicine as a sedative for headaches.

Gomphrena

Common Name: **Globe amaranth**

Availability: May–December.

Vase Life: Approx 10–14 days.

Flower Notes: Pronounced 'Gom-free-na'. Gomphrena is an unusual garden annual with a small, fluffy clover-like flower and attractive grey-green leaves. Medium stem length.

Colour Range: Jewel pink, red.

For the Florist:

- Ideal temperature range 2–5°C (36–41°F).
- Change water every 2–3 days, re-cutting stems each time.
- Prefers to be kept in cool conditions and out of direct sunlight.
- Bunches can become easily tangled, pull apart gently to separate.
- **Stem Type:** Soft.
- **Form:** Round.

For the Home:

- Re-cut stems at an angle and place in clean, fresh water.
- Change water every 2–3 days, re-cutting stems each time and adding flower food.
- Gomphrena make great dried flowers. Remove all foliage and hang upside down in a cool place with good air circulation. They should take about two weeks to dry.
- If using in flower arrangements, two or three heads grouped together will be more effective than if used singly.

 Gomphrena globosa 'Strawberry Fields'

For Weddings:

With the leaves removed, this pretty flower would look lovely in tied posies, where it would complement larger-headed flowers such as Nerines and peonies. In Hawaii they string individual flower heads of Gomphrena together to make leis. Suitable for using in wired work.

For Students:

Family: Amaranthaceae.

Genus: Gomphrena.

Origin: Central America.

Flower Trivia: In Trinidad, Gomphrena flowers are boiled to make tea which is used to treat gripe in babies.

Grevillea

Availability: September–June.

Vase Life: Approx 10–14 days.

Flower Notes: Pronounced 'Gre-VIL-e-la'. A shrubby, sun loving plant with soft, needle-like foliage and flowers which resemble brightly coloured bottle brushes. Medium stem length.

Colour Range: Red, pink, orange, yellow.

For the Florist:

- Ideal temperature range 2–5°C (36–41°F).
- Can be kept up to five days without water.
- Use secateurs to cut stems and add flower food.
- Don't overcrowd vases as flower heads and stems can tangle easily.
- Very sensitive to ethylene gas.
- **Stem Type:** Woody.
- **Form:** Line.

For the Home:

- Re-cut stems at an angle and place in clean, fresh water.
- Flower food is recommended, change water every 2–3 days.
- If arranging in floral foam, keep the container topped up with fresh water.
- For maximum vase life, display in a cool position.
- Grevillea's interesting, spiky form will complement Gerbera, Protea or Alpinia.

 Grevillea 'Misty Red'

For Weddings:

Grevillea is a fun flower although not one that would necessarily be first on the list when it comes to choosing flowers for a wedding. However, its unusual appearance would certainly be a talking point when used in venue designs where it would be ideal as part of a tropical theme.

For Students:

Family: Proteaceae.

Genus: Grevillea.

Origin: Australia.

Flower Trivia: Named in 1804 after Charles Francis Greville, one of the founders of the RHS who for a brief period was the lover of Emma Hart, who later became the mistress of Lord Nelson.

Gypsophila

Common Name: **Gyp, Baby's breath, Maiden's breath**

Availability: All year round.

Vase Life: Approx 7–14 days.

Flower Notes: Pronounced 'Gyp-so-FIL-lee-a'. Although often used simply as a 'filler', Gypsophila is also very effective used as a flower in its own right, particularly in wedding work. Medium stem length.

Colour Range: Pure white, cream, sometimes pink; can be dyed, glittered or painted.

For the Florist:

- Ideal temperature range 5–8°C (41–46°F).
- Keep Gypsophila at room temperature to prevent the flowers from turning brown.
- To prolong vase life, store in daylight at room temperature.
- Very sensitive to ethylene gas, so needs to be in an area with good air circulation.
- **Form:** Transitional.

Gypsophila paniculata
'Million Stars'

For the Home:

- Re-cut stems at an angle and place in clean, fresh water.
- Flower food is important as Gypsophila is prone to bacteria.
- Change water every 2–3 days and remove any leaves in contact with water.
- Suitable for drying, hang upside down in small bunches in an area with good air circulation.
- Some Gypsophila has a sweet scent, but a few varieties are more 'pungent'.

For Weddings:

For a true fairy tale wedding, a bouquet of Gypsophila would have just the right balance of romance and delicacy. It will also bring a touch of feminine softness when added into bridal flowers or wired into corsages. Don't underestimate it!

Flower meaning: Pure of heart.

For Students:

Family: Caryophyllaceae.

Genus: Gypsophila.

Origin: Europe, Asia, North Africa.

Flower Trivia: Gypsophila is in the same botanical family as carnations. It grows on chalky soil, its name literally meaning 'lover of chalk'.

Helenium

Common Name: **Sneezeweed, Helen's flower**

Availability: July–November.

Vase Life: Approx 8–10 days.

Flower Notes: A bushy, daisy-like perennial with a pronounced velvety brown centre surrounded by a swirl of single petals. Medium stem length.

Colour Range: Warm shades of yellow, terracotta and burnt orange.

For the Florist:

- Ideal temperature range 2–5°C (36–41°F).
- Remove all foliage in contact with water.
- Change water every 2–3 days re-cutting stems each time.
- The flower stems can become tangled, pull apart gently to separate them.
- **Form:** Transitional.

For the Home:

- Re-cut stems at an angle and place in clean, fresh water.
- Change water every 2–3 days, and add flower food.
- Helenium would look very pretty in a rustic-style container arranged with herbs such as mint and oregano.

 Helenium 'Kanaria'

For Weddings:

A charming flower that would look lovely in natural tied posies and simple vase designs. Combine Helenium with autumnal flowers in contrasting shapes and colours such as Amaranthus and Achillea for a rich, textural effect. Stems are a little too soft for wired work.

For Students:

Family: Asteraceae.
Genus: Helenium.
Origin: Central and North America.
Flower Trivia: Early American settlers dried Helenium leaves to make snuff, believing that the subsequent sneezing would rid the body of evil spirits.

Helianthus

Common Name: **Sunflower**

Availability: May–October, with limited availability the rest of the year.

Vase Life: Approx 7–10 days.

Flower Notes: A universally loved and instantly recognised flower, with bright single petals arranged around a velvety brown centre. Medium/tall stem length.

Colour Range: Pale yellow, bright yellow, orange, tawny red.

For the Florist:

- Ideal temperature range 8–10°C (46–50°F).
- For maximum vase life store sunflowers at room temperature.
- Re-cut 3cm (2") from bottom of stem, stand in cold water with shrub or flower food.
- Change water every other day, remove unsightly leaves.
- **Form:** Round.

For the Home:

- Re-cut stems at an angle and place in clean, fresh water with flower food.
- Remove any foliage in contact with water which should be changed every other day.
- Get a second life from your sunflower by removing fading petals leaving the attractive brown centre.
- Not recommended for using in floral foam as the stems do not take up water easily.
- To dry, hang the flowers upside down in a cool place with good air circulation. They should take between two to four weeks.

Helianthus annuus 'Sunrich Orange'

For Weddings:

Striking and individual in appearance, sunflowers are a very personal choice of wedding flower. The smaller headed varieties will add a dash of colour to tied posies and table vases while their taller relations would look impressive arranged with strong foliage to show off their beauty. **Flower meaning:** (Tall) Haughtiness, (Small) Adoration.

For Students:

Family: Asteraceae.

Genus: Helianthus.

Origin: USA & Central America.

Flower Trivia: Worshipped by the Incas of Peru due to their resemblance to the life giving sun. The sunflower is also the state flower of Kansas.

Heliconia

Availability: All year round, with limited supply in July and August.

Vase Life: Approx 10–14 days.

Flower Notes: Heliconia is a striking and impressive tropical flower with long oval leaves and beak like waxy bracts which contain tiny flowers. Tall stem length.

Colour Range: Pink, red, yellow, orange.

For the Florist:

- Minimum storage temperature 15°C (59°F).
- Temperatures below 13°C (55°F) can cause flowers to blacken.
- Keep out of direct sun and heat sources to avoid dehydration.
- Mist regularly to keep up humidity and ensure vases are topped up with water.
- Change water every 2–3 days re-cutting stems each time.
- **Form:** Line.

For the Home:

- Re-cut stems at an angle with secateurs and place in clean water with flower food.
- Change water every 2–3 days re-cutting the stems to ensure a flow of water to the flower head.
- Stems are top heavy, so if arranging in floral foam make sure they have plenty of support.
- Display out of direct sunlight and mist gently every day to stop the flower from drying out.

Heliconia stricta

For Weddings:

A dramatic flower, perfect for a wedding in a modern, contemporary venue. Use as a centrepiece in structured designs with equally bold flowers such as Anthuriums, Strelitzias and gingers. If using in vases on tables, make sure the vase is tall and sturdy enough to support the flower.

For Students:

Family: Heliconiaceae.

Genus: Heliconia.

Origin: Tropical Americas and South Pacific.

Flower Trivia: The tiny Honduran white bat lives only in rainforests that contain Heliconia. They make 'tents' out of the large veined leaves to protect themselves from rain and predators.

Helleborus

Common Name: **Hellebore, Christmas rose, Lenten rose**

Availability: November–May.

Vase Life: Approx 5–7 days.

Flower Notes: Brightening up winter gardens when other flowers are dormant, hellebores have an attractive, cup-shaped flower with delicately patterned petals. Short stem length.

Colour Range: Soft white, pale lime, mauve, burgundy.

For the Florist:

- Ideal temperature range 3–5°C (38–41°F).
- Cut approx 2cm (1") from the stem and place immediately in deep, tepid water for 6–8 hours.
- Re-cut stems every other day and use flower food.
- Revive wilting flowers by immersing heads briefly in cold water.
- Hellebores are poisonous, always wash hands after use.
- **Stem Type:** Soft.

For the Home:

- Re-cut stems and place in clean water. A short vertical cut in the stem will improve water absorption.
- Display in a cool position away from direct heat sources.
- Replace water every 2–3 days, misting gently each time.
- Flowers where the seed head has developed will have a longer vase life.
- Arrange with berried ivy and holly for a simple, natural Christmas display.

 Helleborus orientalis

For Weddings:

Hellebores are perfect winter wedding flowers, contrasting beautifully with burgundy and deep greens. Use in tied posies with care as they can have an irritant effect. If arranging in floral foam, keep containers topped up with water. Stems are too fleshy for wiring. **Flower Meaning:** Relieve my anxiety.

For Students:

Family: Ranunculaceae.

Genus: Helleborus.

Origin: Central/Southern Europe.

Flower Trivia: Hellebores have been associated with medicine and magic for centuries. The Ancient Greeks believed them to be a cure for insanity.

Hippeastrum

Common Name: **Amaryllis**

Availability: September–April with limited availability in the summer months.

Vase Life: Approx 10–14 days.

Flower Notes: No one can fail to be impressed by the huge trumpet-shaped blooms of the Hippeastrum. It is commonly (but erroneously) called Amaryllis, a single species flower in the same flower family. Tall stem length.

Colour Range: Pure white, pink, salmon, peach, bright red, deep red, also bicoloured.

For the Florist:

- Ideal temperature range 5–10°C (41–50°F). Lower temperatures can cause the buds to discolour.
- Displaying in opaque vases or wrapping the base of the stems with tape, wool or elastic helps to prevent the ends from 'curling'.
- Wilting flowers can be revived by hanging them upside down and filling the stems with water.
- **Stem Type:** Hollow.
- **Form:** Round.

For the Home:

- Re-cut stems at a 90° angle and place in clean, fresh water.
- If flowers become top heavy, a cane inserted into the hollow stem will help to support them.
- Bulb flower food can be used, but is not essential.
- Closed buds will continue to open; remove old flower heads as they wilt.
- Arrange in a sturdy vase with tall twigs or spiky flowers such as Moluccella.

Hippeastrum 'Rilona'

For Weddings:

This stunning flower would be fantastic for winter and Christmas weddings. Display in venue and church arrangements with bold flowers such as chrysanthemum blooms and gladioli or bind stems together to stand alone in a tall vase as a centrepiece.

Flower Meaning: Splendid beauty.

For Students:

Family: Amaryllidaceae.

Genus: Hippeastrum.

Origin: Central & South America.

Flower Trivia: The Dutch were the first Europeans to develop commercial Hippeastrum from bulbs imported from South America in the eighteenth century.

Hyacinthus

Common Name: **Hyacinth**

Availability: November–May.

Vase Life: Approx 7–10 days.

Flower Notes: A highly fragrant spring flower with waxy, bell-shaped florets packed densely onto thick fleshy stems. Short stem length.

Colour Range: Pure white, cream, salmon, china blue, deep blue, light pink, cerise pink, lilac.

For the Florist:

- Ideal temperature range 2–5°C (36–41°F).
- Prolonged storage in cool conditions can reduce its fragrance.
- Re-cut the bulb end, but don't remove it altogether, this will improve the flowers ability to take up water.
- Can be a skin irritant, so wash hands after use.
- **Stem Type:** Soft.
- **Form:** Line.

Hyacinthus orientalis 'Woodstock'

For the Home:

- Rinse and re-cut stems, leaving as much of the bulb on as possible.
- Stand in clean, fresh, shallow water which should be replaced every other day.
- Use flower food and mist occasionally to prolong vase life.
- If the flowers become top heavy, a thick wire inserted carefully inside the stem will give extra support.
- Hyacinths look lovely arranged in a simple vase or jug. Add in Anemones for an early spring display.

For Weddings:

The delicate shades and sweet scent of hyacinths make them a 'must have' flower for spring weddings. The fleshy stems don't anchor well into floral foam, but in tieds or vase designs they are ideal. Individual florets can be pipped for wired work. **Flower Meaning:** (Pink hyacinth) Playful joy.

For Students:

Family: Asparagaceae.

Genus: Hyacinthus.

Origin: South-West Asia.

Flower Trivia: In Homer's Iliad, Hyacinths were part of the couch of flowers that carried Hera, Queen of Heaven and Earth.

Hydrangea

Common Name: **Hydrangea, Hortensia**

Availability: February–December, peaking May–October.

Vase Life: Approx 7–14 days.

Flower Notes: A cottage garden classic, the showy, unmistakable mop-shaped heads of Hydrangea are, despite their size, hugely versatile. Tall stem length.

Colour Range: Pure white, china blue, deep blue, lilac, light pink, cerise pink, burgundy, green.

For the Florist:

- Ideal temperature range 5–8°C (41–46°F).
- Use secateurs to re-cut stems and remove leaves in contact with water.
- Clean, fresh water is essential for maximum vase life.
- Change water every day, re-cutting stems each time.
- Limp heads can be revived by submerging them for a short period in tepid water.
- **Stem Type:** Woody.
- **Form:** Round.

For the Home:

- Re-cut stems and stand in clean, fresh water with flower food.
- Replace water every day, re-cutting stems each time. Mist occasionally to prolong vase life.
- Hydrangea is easy to dry; remove the leaves and stand the flowers in shallow water in a cool spot. They will gradually dry out as the water evaporates.

 Hydrangea macrophylla 'Diamond Blue'

For Weddings:

A fabulous flower for weddings, adding country chic and a touch of vintage glamour to bridal bouquets, table designs and large arrangements. The delicate blue and pink varieties are ideal for summer weddings, the richer green and burgundy for autumn. **Flower Meaning:** Thank you for understanding.

For Students:

Family: Hydrangeaceae .

Genus: Hydrangea.

Origin: Eastern Asia & USA.

Flower Trivia: Ama-cha is a sweet tea made from dried Hydrangea leaves. It is prepared each year in Japan to celebrate Buddha's birthday.

Hypericum

Common Name: **St. John's Wort, Tutsan, Coffee bean**

Availability: All year round.

Vase Life: Approx 10–14 days.

Flower Notes: A woody herbaceous shrub with bright yellow flowers and prominent stamens which develop into attractive berry-like capsules. Medium stem length.

Colour Range: Cream, lemon, lime green, orange, bright red, amber, reddish brown.

For the Florist:

- Ideal temperature range 2–5°C (36–41°F).
- Remove any foliage in contact with water.
- Change water every 2–3 days re-cutting the stems each time.
- A blast of leaf shine will improve the berries appearance in design work.
- **Stem Type:** Woody.
- **Form:** Transitional.

For the Home:

- Re-cut stems with secateurs and place in clean, fresh water which should be changed every 2–3 days.
- The leaves will wilt before the berries. Remove damaged foliage to improve appearance.
- Immersing stems in tepid water can revive limp foliage.
- An excellent, long-lasting filler flower.
- Arrange the red/brown varieties with rich autumnal shades, the creams and limes with fresh spring colours.

 Hypericum x inodorum 'Excellent Flair'

For Weddings:
Very useful for adding depth and a touch of autumn seasonality to bridal work. Hypericum will also complement larger-headed flowers such as roses and carnations. Small groups of berries wired together add texture to corsages, buttonholes and boutonnières. Has a slight peppery scent.

For Students:
Family: Hypericaceae.
Genus: Hypericum.
Origin: Indigenous to Europe.
Flower Trivia: Ancient Greeks and Romans put sprigs of Hypericum above statues in their homes, in the belief that it would ward off evil spirits.

Ilex

Availability: October–December.

Vase Life: Approx 7–14 days.

Flower Notes: *Ilex verticillata* is a deciduous holly, losing its leaves in late autumn to expose clusters of bright berries on bare stems that last throughout the winter. Medium/tall stem length.

Colour Range: Bright red, deep gold, yellow gold.

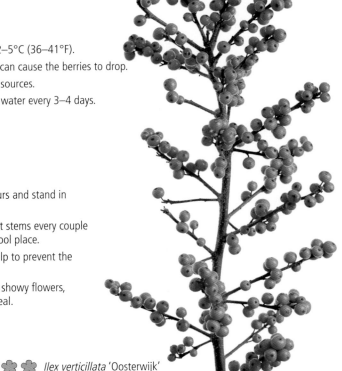

For the Florist:

- Ideal temperature range 2–5°C (36–41°F).
- Exposure to ethylene gas can cause the berries to drop.
- Display out of direct heat sources.
- Re-cut stems and change water every 3–4 days.
- **Stem Type:** Woody.
- **Form:** Line.

For the Home:

- Re-cut stems with secateurs and stand in clean, fresh water.
- To prolong vase life, re-cut stems every couple of days and display in a cool place.
- Applying hairspray can help to prevent the berries from shrivelling.
- Arrange in tall vases with showy flowers, Hippeastrum would be ideal.

 *Ilex verticillata* 'Oosterwijk'

For Weddings:

A must for any bride getting married at Christmas, for not only does Ilex give that essential seasonal touch to designs, it can also be cut into smaller pieces for using in arrangements and wired work. Add it into bridal flowers for a splash of vibrant colour and shiny texture.

Flower Meaning: Domestic happiness.

For Students:

Family: Aquifoliaceae.

Genus: Ilex.

Origin: N. America and S/E Canada.

Flower Trivia: The berries are mildly toxic to humans and animals but are an important source of food for birds that have to wait for the first frosts before the berries are soft enough to eat.

Iris

Common Name: **Dutch Iris, Flag Iris**

Availability: All year round.

Vase Life: Approx 4–7 days.

Flower Notes: Despite its short vase life, Iris remains a popular spring flower with its distinctive 'fan' shape and rich colours. Medium stem length.

Colour Range: White, yellow, pale blue, deep blue, royal purple. All with a distinctive yellow throat.

For the Florist:

- Ideal temperature range 2–5°C (36–41°F).
- If delivered 'dry' re-cut stems, wrap in paper and stand in water for a couple of hours to condition.
- Closed buds can be gently 'teased' open if needed.
- Keep out of direct heat and sunlight for maximum vase life. Ethylene sensitive.
- **Stem Type:** Soft.
- **Form:** Line.

For the Home:

- Re-cut stems and stand in clean, fresh water.
- Flower food is recommended, specifically for bulbs if available.
- To prolong vase life, re-cut stems every couple of days and display in a cool place.
- Arrange with contrasting spring flowers such as Ranunculus, Genista and Forsythia.

Iris 'Blue Magic'

For Weddings:

Due to its angular shape, Iris is not a flower that sits easily in bridal work. Use instead in table arrangements and vase designs where its unique form can be appreciated. A perfect flower for a spring wedding although too soft for using in wired work.

Flower meaning: Faith.

For Students:

Family: Iridaceae.

Genus: Iris.

Origin: Europe and North Africa.

Flower Trivia: In Greek mythology, Iris was the messenger of the Gods, who, clothed in a cloak of raindrops, communicated via a rainbow, the bridge between Heaven and Earth.

Common Name: **African corn lily**

Availability: April–July.

Vase Life: Approx 5–7 days.

Flower Notes: A member of the Iris family, Ixia has pretty star-shaped flowers which are borne in clusters on long slim, wiry stems. Medium stem length.

Colour Range: Pink/white, rose pink, deep pink, red.

For the Florist:

- Ideal temperature range 2–5°C (36–41°F).
- Ixia is very sensitive to the effects of ethylene gas.
- Beware of buying Ixia if it looks immature as the buds may not open.
- Keep out of direct heat sources, and use flower food.
- **Stem Type:** Soft.
- **Form:** Line.

For the Home:

- Re-cut stems and stand in clean, fresh water.
- Change vase water every 2–3 days and add flower food.
- Display in a cool spot out of direct heat and sunshine.
- Complement Ixia with other delicate flowers such as spray roses or Freesia.

 *Ixia* 'Phoenix Rose'

For Weddings:

A pretty, dainty flower to use in a late spring, early summer wedding. Ixia would add line and structure to more formal bouquets, but might get a little lost in tied designs and large arrangements. Suitable for wiring into buttonholes and corsages.

For Students:

Family: Iridaceae.

Genus: Ixia.

Origin: South Africa.

Flower Trivia: Ixia means chameleon plant, as the flower grows in a wide range of colours, the most striking being *Ixia viridiflora*, a brilliant turquoise green. (Sadly not available as a cut flower).

Jasminum

Common Name: **Jasmine**

Availability: November–May as a houseplant with limited availability as a cut flower in that period.

Vase Life: Approx 4–6 days.

Flower Notes: A highly fragrant and often vigorous climber with simple, star-shaped flowers borne in clusters. Very popular as a flowering houseplant. Medium stem length.

Colour Range: Pure white, pale pink.

For the Florist:

- Ideal temperature range 2–5°C (36–41°F).
- Remove any leaves in contact with water and keep away from draughts.
- Jasmines like humidity; mist leaves and flowers gently.
- Prolonged storage in a cold room will reduce its fragrance.
- **Form:** Line/Transitional.

For the Home:

- Re-cut stems and stand in clean, fresh water.
- Mist gently occasionally and display out of direct heat sources and sunlight.
- Not suitable for use in floral foam unless for a very short period (e.g for weddings or competitions).
- The delicate flowers of jasmine would complement smaller-headed flowers such as spray roses or Phlox.

 Jasminum polyanthum

For Weddings:
For brides wishing to use jasmine it may be easier and more economical to buy flowering houseplants and carefully unravel the delicate tendrils to cut and use in bridal work. The plants could then be used to decorate the venue or given as thoughtful presents for guests to take home. Ideal for the budget conscious bride!
Flower meaning: Attachment.

For Students:
Family: Oleaceae.
Genus: Jasminum.
Origin: Himalayas, Western China.
Flower Trivia: Jasmine is grown in large quantities in India where it is has many uses, from hair ornaments to jasmine tea which is believed to have many health benefits, including warding off signs of ageing.

Jatropha

Common Name: **Guatemalan rhubarb, Barbados nut**

Availability: All year round, in small quantities only.

Vase Life: Approx 10–14 days.

Flower Notes: Pronounced 'JAT-tro-fuh'. A tropical succulent with an unusual, coral-like appearance and large lobed, waxy leaves. Tough and robust it has a distinctive swollen, club shaped base. Medium stem length.

Colour Range: Scarlet with bright green fruits.

For the Florist:

- Ideal temperature range 8–12°C (46–54°F).
- Use secateurs or a sharp knife to re-cut the thick, fleshy stems.
- Susceptible to bacteria, use a clean vase and change water every other day.
- Try to avoid any damage to the stem as this could allow rot to set in.
- **Form:** Transitional.

For the Home:

- Re-cut stems and stand in clean, fresh water which should be changed every other day.
- Display at room temperature but away from direct heat.
- The tiny red tips break off if dry or damaged, handle with care.
- In warm conditions it will continue to develop, revealing bright yellow flowers.
- To show off this striking flower, display three or five stems in a simple vase against a plain background.

Jatropha podagrica

For Weddings:

Tropical flowers are not usually the first port of call for a bride, but if there is an occasion where the colour scheme is for hot colours with a modern theme, Jatropha would be high on the list. Its distinctive colouring with the lime green fruits perhaps lends itself more to an autumn wedding. Unsuitable for wiring.

For Students:

Family: Euphorbiaceae.

Genus: Jatropha

Native to: Tropical Americas.

Flower Trivia: A specialised hot house plant, popular with succulent collectors, one of Jatrophas more descriptive common names (and my favourite) is Gouty Stalk Nettle Spurge.

Kniphofia

Common Name: **Red-hot poker, Torch lily, Poker plant**

Availability: April–September.

Vase Life: Approx 7–10 days.

Flower Notes: Pronounced 'Knee-pho-fia'. A popular garden plant whose common names accurately sum up its bright, rocket-shaped flowers which brighten up borders in late summer and early autumn. Medium stem length.

Colour Range: Vibrant orange, pale orange, yellow, bright green.

For the Florist:

- Ideal temperature range 8–10°C (46–50°F).
- Store upright as stem ends will naturally turn upwards if lying flat.
- Sensitive to ethylene gas. Stand in a cool place away from possible sources.
- Re-cut stems every 2–3 days to maintain a flow of water to the flower head.
- Form: Line.

For the Home:

- Re-cut stems with a knife and stand in clean, fresh water.
- Flower food is recommended and water should be changed every 2–3 days, re-cutting stems each time.
- Remove individual flowers as they die on the stem.
- This is a great autumn flower; arrange with strong colours and bold shapes – Aconitum, Dahlia or Chrysanthemum blooms.

 Kniphofia 'Alcazar'

For Weddings:

The stems are really too chunky for bridal flowers, but Kniphofia would look impressive grouped in large designs for churches or receptions. If arranging in vases, ensure they are wide and heavy enough to hold the thick stems. Ideal for late summer, early autumn ceremonies.

For Students:

Family: Asphodelaceae.

Genus: Kniphofia.

Origin: Africa.

Flower Trivia: The nectar within the flowers is very attractive to birds, particularly sparrows, who can strip a stem clean in minutes.

Lathyrus

Common Name: **Sweet pea, Everlasting pea**

Availability: March–August, peaks April–July.

Vase Life: Approx 5–10 days.

Flower Notes: Its butterfly-shaped petals, delicate shades and intensely sweet fragrance have made the sweet pea one of the nation's favourite summer flowers. Simply irresistible. Short stem length.

Colour Range: White, cream, pale blue, lilac, purple, pale pink, cerise pink, burgundy.

For the Florist:

- Ideal temperature range 8–10°C (46–50°F).
- Cooler temperatures can reduce fragrance and potentially mark the flowers.
- Stand in shallow water as hairs on the stem cause water to creep upwards, encouraging botrytis.
- Do not mist or expose to temperature fluctuations, as these can cause damage to petals.
- Very sensitive to ethylene gas.
- **Stem Type:** Soft/Hairy.
- **Form:** Line.

For the Home:

- Re-cut stems and stand in clean, fresh shallow water.
- Flower food is recommended and water should be changed every other day.
- Stand in a cool spot, out of direct heat sources with good air circulation.
- Arrange with other delicate flowers such as Ranunculus, Alchemilla or spray roses.

Lathyrus odoratus
'Misty Lavendel'

For Weddings:

The soft texture and sweet fragrance of sweet peas make them a very popular bridal flower. Perfect for tied posies and vases as although their stems are strong enough for floral foam, they prefer to be in water. Can be wired, but handle with care as the delicate flowers bruise easily.

Flower meaning: Blissful pleasure.

For Students:

Family: Papilionaceae.

Genus: Lathyrus.

Origin: Central/Southern Europe.

Flower Trivia: The Shropshire town of Wem is known as the home of the modern sweet pea, which was developed by local nurseryman Henry Eckford in 1887.

Lavandula

Common Name: **Lavender**

Availability: March–May as a fresh flower. Dried - all year round.

Vase Life: Approx 5–10 days.

Flower Notes: A popular evergreen shrub with true cottage garden charm. Its fragrant flowers are used extensively in herbal medicine and beauty products. Medium stem length.

Colour Range: Grey/blue, purple.

For the Florist:

- Ideal temperature range 5–8°C (41–46°F).
- Cooler temperatures may reduce its fragrance.
- Lavender needs good air circulation to stop stems from becoming mouldy.
- Do not mist, as this will only make the flower soggy.
- Don't overcrowd containers; water should be changed daily.
- **Form:** Line.

For the Home:

- Re-cut stems with scissors and stand in clean, fresh water.
- Remove all foliage in contact with water and add flower food.
- Keep out of direct heat sources and change water daily.
- Lavender can be air dried by hanging upside down in small bundles (so ensuring air can reach the centre) in a cool, dry spot. It should take between 2 to 3 weeks.

Lavandula angustifolia 'Hidcote'

For Weddings:

Lavender will add scent and texture to tied posies and venue designs and is particularly suitable for brides wanting that natural, 'just picked' look. Fresh lavender will give extra depth to spring flowers, dried lavender a seasonal richness to autumnal designs. Its intense fragrance may upset hay fever sufferers.

Flower meaning: Love, devotion.

For Students:

Family: Lamiaceae.

Genus: Lavandula.

Origin: Mediterranean.

Flower Trivia: Lavender has a history going back 3,000 years. Its name comes from the Latin 'lavare' meaning to wash; from the same stem comes the word 'laundry'.

Leucadendron

Common Name: **Safari sunset, Flame tip**

Availability: All year round, with different varieties peaking within that period.

Vase Life: Approx 14–28 days.

Flower Notes: A bushy, evergreen shrub with stiff, waxy leaves. The flower itself is insignificant; it's the showy bracts around it which provide Leucadendrons striking colour combinations. Medium/tall stem length.

Colour Range: Sage green, lime green, burgundy, orange.

For the Florist:

- Ideal temperature range 5–8°C (41–46°F).
- Remove foliage in contact with water and change water every 4–5 days.
- Any tightly closed bracts will not open further once the flower has been cut.
- Keep out of direct heat sources as this can cause the leaves to blacken.
- **Stem Type:** Woody.
- **Form:** Line.

For the Home:

- Re-cut stems with secateurs and stand in clean, fresh water.
- Change water every 4–5 days, flower food is recommended.
- Stand in a cool spot and remove any foliage in contact with water.
- Arrange with vibrant flowers in bold shapes; red Anthuriums or orange Gerberas would be perfect.

 Leucadendron x 'Safari Sunset'

For Weddings:
The tall striking stems of Leucadendron would be very suitable for large designs in venues and for adding texture to tied posies and bouquets. Team up the burgundy shades with oranges, reds and gold for an autumn wedding, the lime varieties with creams, yellows and whites for spring or summer.

For Students:
Family: Proteaceae.
Genus: Leucadendron.
Origin: South Africa.
Flower Trivia: *Leucadendron x* 'Safari Sunset' is a hybrid of *L. Laureolum* and *L. Salignum* and is one of the best known Leucadendrons, exported as a cut flower from a number of countries.

Leucanthemum

Common Name: **Shasta daisy**

Availability: May–August.

Vase Life: Approx 10–14 days.

Flower Notes: A daisy-like herbaceous plant which makes an excellent cut flower. 'Wirral Supreme' is the double variety most commonly available commercially. Medium stem length.

Colour Range: Pure white with a bright yellow centre.

For the Florist:

- Ideal temperature range 2–8°C (36–46°F).
- Needs good air circulation and a cool spot for maximum vase life.
- Re-cut stems and change water every 3–4 days.
- They emit large amounts of ethylene gas, so keep away from ethylene sensitive flowers.
- **Form:** Round.

For the Home:

- Re-cut stems and place in clean, fresh water with flower food.
- Remove all foliage in contact with water and change water every 3–4 days.
- If cutting straight from the garden, stand the flower in deep water for a few hours before using.
- Arrange with bright, summery flowers such as Delphiniums, Eremurus or Nigella.

 Leucanthemum x superbum
'Snow Lady'

For Weddings:

For old-fashioned vintage style, team this pure white daisy with lemons, oranges or blues. Arrange them in simple bunches in pretty containers for a fresh, summery look. They would look particularly effective arranged with grasses and lime coloured flowers such as *Alchemilla mollis*.

For Students:

Family: Asteraceae.

Genus: Leucanthemum.

Origin: Europe.

Flower Trivia: American botanist Luther Burbank developed the Shasta daisy in part from wild flowers brought to the US by the Pilgrim Fathers.

Leucospermum

Common Name: **Pincushion protea, Nodding pincushion, Sunburst protea**

Availability: All year, with different varieties peaking within that period.

Vase Life: Approx 10–15 days.

Flower Notes: It's not difficult to see the origin of the common name of this woody shrub. Indigenous to South Africa it has tough leathery leaves which grow in a spiral below the spiky flower head. Medium stem length.

Colour Range: Tawny orange, bright red, yellow, gold.

For the Florist:

- Ideal temperature range 2–5°C (36–41°F).
- Needs good air circulation to avoid flower heads becoming rotten.
- Encourage water to flow to the head by frequently re-cutting stems.
- Remove all foliage in contact with water.
- Handle carefully – the heads can easily be knocked off.
- **Stem Type:** Woody.
- **Form:** Round.

For the Home:

- Re-cut stems with secateurs and stand in clean, fresh water.
- Remove all foliage below the water line. Flower food is recommended.
- Stand in a cool spot, out of direct heat sources with good air circulation.
- Arrange with bold, textural flowers such as Dahlias, Kniphofias or Proteas.

 Leucospermum nutans 'High Gold'

For Weddings:
Leucospermum will provide strong textural notes to autumnal colour schemes. As the heads can drop off if knocked, they are best avoided in tied designs. Use instead in compact, grouped arrangements with bold foliages. They last well in floral foam.

For Students:
Family: Proteaceae.
Genus: Leucospermum.
Origin: South Africa.
Flower Trivia: Leucospermum nectar is very attractive to birds and insects, including the specialist nectar feeder, the Cape sugarbird.

Liatris

Common Name: **Gay feather, Button snakewort, Blazing star**

Availability: All year round.

Vase Life: Approx 7–10 days.

Flower Notes: Liatris is a hardy garden perennial with tiny, vivid flowers that grow closely together on an erect spike with very slim, narrow leaves. Medium/tall stem length.

Colour Range: White, violet, purple.

For the Florist:

- Ideal temperature range 2–5°C (36–41°F).
- Don't overcrowd vases, as Liatris needs good air circulation.
- Remove all foliage below water level and change water every other day.
- Susceptible to botrytis; clean containers and fresh water are essential.
- Form: Line.

For the Home:

- Re-cut stems and stand in clean, fresh water with flower food.
- Change water every 2–3 days, re-cutting stems each time.
- Liatris foliage can become black and slimy if in contact with water, so it's important to remove all leaves below the water line.
- Flowers will open from the top downwards.
- Air dry Liatris when two-thirds of flowers are open, by hanging them upside down in small bunches.
- Contrast with bright, round flowers; sunflowers, Chrysanthemum blooms or Alliums.

 Liatris spicata

For Weddings:

Not a flower you would normally expect to see in a bridal bouquet, but it would fit happily into a purple/pink colour scheme and add texture and line to church and venue arrangements. Liatris lasts well in floral foam. Use this spiky flower in more structured designs to make the most of its linear shape.

For Students:

Family: Asteraceae.

Genus: Liatris.

Origin: Eastern USA.

Flower Trivia: Prairie Blazing Star *(Liatris pycnostachya)* a native to the state of Missouri, is the tallest of the genus, growing up to 152cm (5ft) in height.

Lilium

Lilium asiatica 'Red Latin'

Availability: All year round.

Vase Life: Approx 10–14 days.

Flower Notes: Never out of the top ten of the world's best selling cut flowers it is the Asiatic, Longiflorum and Oriental lilies that are commercially the most popular. The Oriental is the most heavily scented of the three. Tall stem length.

Colour Range: All colours from pure white to deep burgundy with the exception of green and blue.

For the Florist:

- Ideal temperature range 2–5°C (41–46°F).
- Lower temperatures can damage blooms and turn buds brown.
- Remove all leaves in contact with water and use flower food.
- If delivered dry, re-cut stems and stand in deep water to condition.
- Remove the stamens when the flowers open to prevent staining clients and customers!
- **Form:** Round/Transitional.

For the Home:

- Re-cut stems and stand in clean, fresh water with flower food.
- Remove the stamens to prevent staining; this will not shorten the life of the flower.
- Remove pollen stains by brushing gently or by using sticky tape. Avoid water, this will only make things worse!
- Lilies are poisonous, particularly to cats, where ingestion of any part of the flower can be fatal.

For Weddings:

Lilies look fabulous in large, showy bouquets and are equally impressive in vase designs and arrangements. Choose the unscented varieties if anyone in the bridal party suffers from hay fever. A little too delicate for wiring work as the flowers bruise easily.

Flower meaning: Majesty and honour.

For Students:

Family: Liliaceae.

Genus: Lilium.

Origin: Northern hemisphere.

Flower Trivia: In China, lily bulbs are commonly used as an ingredient in stir-fries, soups and cold dishes.

Lilium

Common Name: **Longi, Easter/trumpet lily**

Availability: All year round.

Vase Life: Approx 10–14 days.

Flower Notes: A bulbous perennial with strap-like leaves and unmistakable waxy, trumpet shaped flowers, the longiflorum is one of the most popular and recognisable members of the lily family. Tall stem length.

Colour Range: Pure white, pale pink, lemon, also bicoloured.

For the Florist:

- Ideal temperature range 2–5°C (41–46°F).
- Avoid storing/displaying in extremes of temperatures and draughts.
- Usually delivered on dry stems, recut and place into deep, fresh water on arrival.
- Remove all leaves in contact with water and use flower food.
- **Form:** Round/Transitional.

For the Home:

- Re-cut stems with a knife and stand in clean, fresh water with flower food.
- Display at room temperature but away from direct heat which can dry out buds.
- All lilies are poisonous to cats; the longiflorum is especially so, keep well out of the way of pets.
- Buy at Easter and display in a tall vase with stems of pussy willow for a striking, seasonal display.

Lilium longiflorum

For Weddings:

Not such a popular choice for weddings as you might think, although it should certainly be considered for church and reception flowers especially in the spring and at Easter. Equally lovely for large, showy pedestal arrangements or more limited, modern designs, it has a sweet scent and stamens deep enough inside the flower for them not to stain.

Flower Meaning: Pure and honest.

For Students:

Family: Liliaceae.

Genus: Lilium.

Native to: Japan & the Philippines.

Flower Trivia: The Californian/Oregon border in the US is known as the 'Easter Lily Capital of the World', growing 95% of the world's production.

114

Limonium

Common Name: **Statice, Sea lavender**

Availability: All year round.

Vase Life: Approx 10–14 days.

Flower Notes: A dependable, but somewhat old-fashioned garden flower, with two varieties available commercially, the wispy *L. sinensis*, and the more substantial *L. sinuatum*. Medium stem length.

Colour Range: Cream, lemon, yellow, lilac, pink, blue, purple.

For the Florist:

- Ideal temperature range 2–8°C (36–46°F).
- Limonium needs good air circulation, so don't overcrowd vases and containers.
- Can be a water polluter, so change water daily and use flower food.
- *Limonium sinensis* can have a slightly off-putting odour so use sparingly in contract/corporate work.
- **Form:** Transitional.

For the Home:

- Re-cut stems and stand in clean, fresh water.
- Change water every day, adding flower food each time.
- Stand in a cool spot, out of direct heat sources with good air circulation.
- Dry Limonium by standing it in a vase of clean, shallow water in a cool spot. As the water gradually evaporates the flowers will dry out.
- Use Limonium to fill out vases with larger-headed flowers such as roses or sunflowers.

 *Limonium sinuatum* 'Blue Star'

For Weddings:

Not a flower commonly associated with wedding work, although the deep purple varieties will complement rich reds, burgundies and gold. Equally suitable to use in floral foam or in vases, it can also be wired for boutonnières and corsages.

For Students:

Family: Plumbaginaceae.

Genus: Limonium.

Origin: Northern hemisphere.

Flower Trivia: Limonium comes from the ancient Greek 'leimon' meaning meadow.

Lupinus

Common Name: **Lupin, Lupines, Bluebonnet**

Availability: February, May and June.

Vase Life: Approx 5–7 days.

Flower Notes: An old-fashioned cottage garden favourite with tall spires of compact pea-shaped flowers and soft, fan-like leaves. Grows prolifically in the wild. Tall stem length.

Colour Range: Pale blue, purple, pink, cerise pink, burgundy, cream, yellow.

For the Florist:

- Ideal temperature range 2–5°C (36–41°F).
- Display out of draughts and direct heat sources.
- Change water every other day, re-cutting stems each time, and add flower food.
- Reduce the possibility of air locks in the stem by cutting under water.
- **Stem Type:** Hollow.
- **Form:** Line.

For the Home:

- Re-cut stems and stand in clean, fresh water.
- Flower food is recommended and water should be changed every other day, re-cutting stems each time.
- Stand in a cool spot, out of direct heat sources.
- Lupins will look tremendous arranged on their own in a simple, tall container.

  Lupinus polyphyllus

For Weddings:

Ideal for a bride looking for a touch of elegant country chic, lupins will add soft lines and a natural elegance to large designs in churches and venues, especially when teamed up with similar summer flowers such as Delphiniums and peonies.

Flower meaning: Imagination.

For Students:

Family: Papilionaceae.

Genus: Lupinus.

Origin: USA, Mediterranean, Africa.

Flower Trivia: The name lupin stems from the Latin word, 'lupinus' which means wolf, as it was thought that when growing in large numbers lupines 'ravaged' the soil.

Lysimachia

Common Name: **Loosestrife**

Availability: June–September.

Vase Life: Approx 10–14 days.

Flower Notes: Pronounced 'LYE-sis-mac-e-a'. A pretty herbaceous perennial native to damp meadows and wetlands, Lysimachia is also a common sight in many gardens in the summer. Medium stem length.

Colour Range: Bright yellow, white, violet, purple.

For the Florist:

- Ideal temperature range 2–5°C (36–41°F).
- Avoid displaying in direct heat sources as this will dry out the flowers.
- They are thirsty flowers, so top up vases and containers regularly.
- Sensitive to ethylene gas, display in an area with good air circulation.
- **Form:** Transitional/Line.

For the Home:

- Re-cut stems and stand in clean, fresh water.
- Remove all foliage below the water line and add flower food.
- Change water every 3–4 days, re-cutting stems each time.
- Stand in a cool spot, out of direct heat sources.
- For a seasonal display arrange with summer flowers such as *Ammi visnaga* or cornflowers.

 Lysimachia vulgaris

For Weddings:

A cheerful flower, perfect for an informal summer wedding, Lysimachia lasts well in floral foam and will add line and structure to larger arrangements. Use in simple vase designs for a country feel. Lysimachia works especially well when added to a lemon, white and lime colour scheme.

For Students:

Family: Primulaceae.

Genus: Lysimachia.

Origin: Europe & North Asia.

Flower Trivia: Part of herbal medicine for over 2,000 years, it was believed that burning loosestrife inside dwellings was an effective way to repel insects.

Matthiola

Common Name: **Stocks, Gillyflower**

Availability: January–August, peaks March–July.

Vase Life: Approx 5–7 days.

Flower Notes: Pronounced 'Ma-the-OH-la'. A highly fragrant cottage garden favourite, stocks are covered with flowers that have a soft, tactile appearance, almost like small rosettes of fabric. Medium stem length.

Colour Range: White, cream, lilac, purple, pale pink, cerise pink, burgundy.

For the Florist:

- Ideal temperature range 2–5°C (36–41°F).
- Cut away any white parts of the stem as they will not take up water.
- Stand in shallow water as 'knuckles' on the stem can let in bacteria.
- Remove all leaves in contact with water, which should be changed every day.
- Wilting flowers can be revived by submerging briefly in tepid water.
- **Stem Type:** Soft.
- **Form:** Line.

 Matthiola incana 'Arabella'

For the Home:

- Re-cut stems and stand in clean, fresh shallow water.
- Use flower food and change water daily as stocks can pollute water, especially in warm weather.
- Stand in a cool spot out of direct heat sources with good air circulation.
- Stocks look gorgeous simply arranged on their own or try with peonies and *Alchemilla mollis*.

For Weddings:
Everything about the soft colour palette and sweet fragrance of stocks says 'wedding flower'. Perfect for tied posies and vase designs, although handle with care, as the flowers can be easily broken off. Stocks don't last well in floral foam and are too soft for wiring.
Flower meaning: Bonds of affection.

For Students:
Family: Brassicaceae.
Genus: Matthiola.
Origin: Mediterranean.
Flower Trivia: Stocks were popular in Elizabethan gardens, where their spicy fragrance led them to be called 'gillyflower' a popular name for any flower with a strong, clove like scent.

Mentha

Common Name: **Mint**

Availability: May–October, peaks June–September.

Vase Life: Approx 7–14 days.

Flower Notes: A popular perennial herb with spikes of tiny flowers standing above soft, highly aromatic leaves. A common sight in many gardens, mint has a wide variety of culinary uses. Medium stem length.

Colour Range: Purple, lilac/silvery grey, pale lilac.

For the Florist:

- Ideal temperature range 2–5°C (36–41°F).
- Remove all leaves in contact with water and change water every 3–4 days.
- If flowers start to wilt, re-cut stems and stand in a refrigeration unit or cool spot for a few hours.
- **Stem Type:** Soft.
- **Form:** Transitional.

For the Home:

- Re-cut stems and stand in clean, fresh water.
- Flower food is recommended and water should be changed every 3–4 days.
- Mint commercially grown for the flower industry may be treated with chemicals so avoid using in cooking.
- Arrange with scented summer flowers; Phlox, spray roses or peonies for an aromatic display.

 Mentha spicata 'Purple Sensation'

For Weddings:

Include mint in natural tied posies with scabious, Nigella and similar herbs such as oregano. Perfect in table vases, but its delicate shape may get a little lost in larger arrangements. Leaves are generally too soft for wiring, but the spikes of flowers can be used in wired work with care.

Flower meaning: Virtue.

For Students:

Family: Lamiaceae.

Genus: Mentha.

Origin: Distributed world wide.

Flower Trivia: Peppermint (*Mentha piperita*) is the most popular of all mints; its fresh, clean taste is the basis of many toothpastes, mouthwashes and soaps.

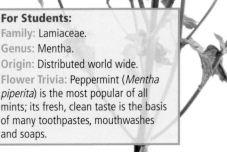

Moluccella

Common Name: **Bells of Ireland, Shell flower**

Availability: All year round.

Vase Life: Approx 8–10 days.

Flower Notes: Pronounced 'Moll-U-sella'. Hooded calyces arranged on tall spikes give this border perennial its distinctive shape. Hidden inside each calyx is a tiny white, fragrant flower. Tall stem length.

Colour Range: Apple green.

For the Florist:

- Ideal temperature range 2–5°C (36–41°F).
- Pinch out the leaves at the top of the spike to improve the flower's appearance.
- Remove all leaves in contact with water and re-cut stems every other day.
- Handle with care as there are small, sharp thorns hidden underneath each calyx.
- **Stem Type:** Hollow.
- **Form:** Line.

For the Home:

- Re-cut stems and stand in clean, fresh water with flower food.
- Remove all foliage below the water line and change water every 1–2 days.
- Moluccella are phototropic so will naturally bend towards the light.
- Some people have a reaction to the tiny spikes on the stem, wear gloves if necessary.
- The flowers can be dried by hanging upside down in small bunches in an airy space.

 Moluccella laevis

For Weddings:
Moluccella is excellent for adding line to large venue arrangements and is equally versatile in traditional or structural designs. A popular flower for Irish celebrations due to its common name. Because of small thorns, not suitable for hand-held designs.
Flower Meaning: Good Luck.

For Students:
Family: Lamiaceae.
Genus: Moluccella.
Origin: Western Asia & Eastern Europe.
Flower Trivia: Cultivated since 1570, Moluccella is named after the Moluccas or Spice islands in Indonesia where it was erroneously thought to originate.

Monarda

Common Name: **Red bergamot, Bee balm**

Availability: June–July.

Vase Life: Approx 7–10 days.

Flower Notes: A perennial from the prairies of North America, Monarda has a tufted flower not dissimilar to a jester's hat. When crushed the leaves exude a spicy, fragrant oil. Medium stem length.

Colour Range: Scarlet, pink.

Monarda didyma 'Red Fountain'

For the Florist:

- Ideal temperature range 2–5°C (36–41°F).
- Re-cut stems and remove all leaves in contact with water.
- Change water every 3–4 days, re-cutting stems and adding flower food.
- These are thirsty flowers, so check water levels regularly.
- **Form:** Round.

For the Home:

- Re-cut stems and stand in clean, fresh water with flower food.
- Change water every 3–4 days, re-cutting stems each time.
- Stand in a cool spot, out of direct heat sources.
- Despite its common name, Monarda is not the source of bergamot oil. This is obtained from the fruit *Citrus aurantium*.
- Arrange with tall, strongly-coloured flowers, such as Aconitum, Eremurus or Moluccella.

For Weddings:
This would be an interesting choice of flower for a wedding, its informal style lending itself to a country garden theme. Choose a bold colour scheme to best emphasise its vivid colour and unusual shape. For maximum impact, use grouped in large designs or arrange in tall vases with flamboyant flowers and foliage.

For Students:
Family: Lamiaceae.

Genus: Monarda.

Origin: North America.

Flower Trivia: Oswego Indians made tea out of powered Monarda. This became a welcome substitute for the real thing after the shortage following the Boston Tea Party in 1773.

Muscari

Common Name: **Grape hyacinth**

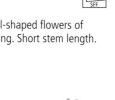

Availability: January–June, peaks February–April.

Vase Life: Approx 4–8 days.

Flower Notes: A bulb which naturalises easily in the garden, the tiny bell-shaped flowers of Muscari are a familiar and welcome sight in the early spring. Short stem length.

Colour Range: Pale blue, violet blue, china blue.

For the Florist:

- Ideal temperature range 2–5°C (36–41°F).
- Cool conditions will hold back the opening of the flower.
- Use specialist bulb or flower food, display in shallow water.
- Wilting flowers can be revived by submerging them briefly in tepid water.
- **Stem Type:** Soft.
- **Form:** Line.

For the Home:

- Re-cut stems with scissors and stand in clean, fresh water.
- Flower food is recommended, one specifically for bulb flowers if possible.
- Stand in a cool spot, out of direct heat sources with good air circulation.
- Arrange in small vases or jugs with white hellebores, Ranunculus or tulips.

 Muscari 'Cupido'

For Weddings:
Such a pretty, delicate flower would be almost impossible to ignore when choosing flowers for a spring bride. Perfect for tied posies and for simple, vintage-style table vases, it will also hold up reasonably well in wired work. Not recommended for using in floral foam.

For Students:
Family: Asparagaceae.
Genus: Muscari.
Origin: Southern Europe, Asia.
Flower Trivia: *Muscari comosum* or tassel hyacinth, is raised as an edible plant in the Mediterranean where it is a popular ingredient in cookery.

Myosotis

Common Name: **Forget-me-not**

Availability: February–April.

Vase Life: Approx 4–6 days.

Flower Notes: Pronounced 'My-oh-SO-tis'. A popular cottage garden perennial which naturalises and spreads easily, creating an unmistakeable carpet of tiny bright blue flowers in the late spring. Short stem length.

Colour Range: Sky blue, pale blue, white.

For the Florist:

- Ideal temperature range 2–5°C (36–41°F).
- Stand in shallow water to prevent the stems from becoming slimy.
- Remove all leaves in contact with water and change water daily.
- Display in a cool spot with good air circulation.
- **Stem Type:** Soft.

For the Home:

- Re-cut stems and stand in clean, fresh, shallow water.
- Flower food is recommended and water should be changed daily.
- The bright colours of the flowers will fade as they age.
- Keep it very simple with Myosotis; try displaying it with white Narcissi or pink tulips.

 Myosotis sylvatica 'Blue Ball'

For Weddings:
Although too dainty and tiny to use in large arrangements, Myosotis would be a poignant addition to small tied designs. Combine it with delicate spring flowers in pretty vases for ultimate country style. The stems are a little too soft for wiring work.
Flower Meaning: True Love.

For Students:
Family: Boraginaceae.
Genus: Myosotis.
Origin: Europe & N. Asia.
Flower Trivia: Its botanical name comes from ancient Greek for 'mouse ear' a reference to its tiny grey leaves. Alpine Forget-me-not is the state flower of Alaska.

123

Narcissus

Common Name: **Daffodil, Jonquil**

Availability: November–May, peaks January–March.

Vase Life: Approx 5–7 days.

Flower Notes: Immortalised in poetry by Wordsworth, spring just wouldn't be the same without the bold, cheerful daffodil. Short stem length.

Colour Range: Pure white, butter cream, pale yellow, bright yellow, gold. Also bicoloured.

For the Florist:

- Ideal temperature range 2–5°C (36–41°F).
- Daffodils that arrive dry can be left for 3–5 days without water at a temperature of 1°C (34°F).
- Always wash scissors and knives after use to remove any traces of sap and wash hands thoroughly.
- Keep out of direct sunlight and heat sources.
- **Stem Type:** Hollow.
- **Form:** Round.

 Narcissus 'Martinette'

For the Home:

- Narcissus exudes toxic sap which can affect other flowers. To overcome this, after re-cutting stems, stand flowers in cold water for 24 hours before adding into designs. Repeat this process every time stems are re-cut.
- Flower food is not recommended, as this encourages the sap to flow.
- Stand in a cool spot out of direct heat sources to maximise vase life.

For Weddings:

Delicate, scented Narcissi are perfect for seasonal spring tied posies. Ensure stems are thoroughly dry before use as the sap can be an irritant. Simple vases filled with cheerful daffodils are an inexpensive and charming way to decorate tables.

Flower meaning: You're the only one.

For Students:

Family: Amaryllidaceae.

Genus: Narcissus.

Origin: Europe & Asia.

Flower Trivia: The Isles of Scilly in Cornwall pay a rent to the Duchy of Cornwall of one daffodil a year for all of its uninhabited islands.

Nerine

Availability: Peaks August–December, limited availability January–July.

Vase Life: Approx 12–14 days.

Flower Notes: An autumnal flowering bulb with a slim single stem that supports a floral firework of vivid flowers with graceful turned-back petals. Medium stem length.

Colour Range: Pure white, pale pink, bubblegum pink, scarlet, deep red.

For the Florist:

- Ideal temperature range 5–8°C (41–46°F).
- Storing in lower temperatures can cause the flowers to turn blue and may also prevent them from opening.
- Use flower food for bulbs if available, and change vase water every 3–4 days.
- **Stem Type:** Soft.
- **Form:** Transitional.

For the Home:

- Re-cut stems and stand in clean, fresh water.
- Flower food is recommended, and water should be changed every 3–4 days.
- Remove the brown outer casing of the flower head to improve its appearance.
- Arrange with roses for a classic look, or lime and purple flowers for something a little more contemporary.

Nerine 'Ras van Roon'

For Weddings:

The straight stems and striking heads of Nerines make them equally effective in modern structured designs or large traditional arrangements. They will add a girly frilliness to tied bouquets, and are quite happy arranged in floral foam or vases. Individual flowers are light enough to be wired and used in corsages and boutonnières.

For Students:

Family: Amaryllidaceae.

Genus: Nerine.

Origin: South Africa.

Flower Trivia: Legend has it that the Nerine came to Guernsey as a result of a shipwreck in the 1600's. *Nerine sarniensis* is the island's national flower.

125

Nigella

Common Name: **Love-in-a-mist, Devil in the bush**

Availability: April–October.

Vase Life: Approx 7–10 days.

Flower Notes: Nigella is a charming, pretty annual with a delicate flower head supported by a cobweb of feathery leaves. Medium stem length.

Colour Range: White, pale blue, sky blue, pale pink.

For the Florist:

- Ideal temperature range 2–5°C (36–41°F).
- Remove all leaves in contact with water and change water daily, adding flower food each time.
- Don't overcrowd containers as this can cause the stems to become slimy.
- **Stem Type:** Soft.
- **Form:** Transitional.

For the Home:

- Re-cut stems and stand in clean, shallow water.
- Flower food is recommended, and water should be changed every day as Nigella is a water polluter.
- Stand in a cool spot, out of direct heat sources with good air circulation.
- The flowers and fruit heads of Nigella can be easily dried by hanging upside down in small bunches in an area with good air circulation.
- For a wild summer meadow effect arrange Nigella with cornflower, Origanum and mint.

Nigella damascena 'Miss Jekyll'

For Weddings:

A pretty flower for a wedding with a soft colour palette that would add a gentle contrast to delicate pinks and creams, and a romantic wispiness to tied bridal designs and vases. The seed heads of Nigella can be wired into corsages and boutonnières.

Flower Meaning: You puzzle me.

For Students:

Family: Ranunculaceae.

Genus: Nigella.

Origin: S. Europe/N. Africa/SW. Asia.

Flower Trivia: Popular in gardens since Elizabethan times, the black seeds of *Nigella sativa* or black cumin are a popular herbal remedy and spice.

Origanum

Common Name: **Oregano, Wild marjoram**

Availability: May–November, peaks June–September.

Vase Life: Approx 7–10 days.

Flower Notes: A popular aromatic herb with grey/green leaves topped by clusters of tiny flowers which give off a pungent scent when crushed. Very useful in herbal medicine as well as in the kitchen. Medium stem length.

Colour Range: Pale pink, deep pink, crimson.

For the Florist:

- Ideal temperature range 2–5°C (36–41°F).
- Remove all leaves in contact with water.
- Change water every other day, adding flower food each time.
- Keep out of the sun and direct heat sources as this will dry out the flower prematurely.
- **Form:** Transitional.

Origanum tyttanthum 'Rose Charm'

For the Home:

- Re-cut stems and stand in clean, fresh water, removing any leaves below the water line.
- Flower food is recommended, and water should be changed every other day.
- Oregano commercially grown for the flower industry may be treated with chemicals so avoid using in cooking.
- Arrange with stocks, scabious or roses in a simple container for a scented, summery display.

For Weddings:

A perfect accompaniment to any selection of natural flowers and foliages, indeed for any bride looking for a traditional English cottage garden look. Oregano will blend beautifully in hand-tied posies and is sturdy enough to use in vases and in floral foam.

Flower meaning: Joy and happiness.

For Students:

Family: Lamiaceae.

Genus: Origanum.

Origin: Mediterranean, Central Asia.

Flower Trivia: Oregano is a natural antiseptic and is sometimes used in the form of an essential oil to lessen the pain of toothache.

Ornithogalum

Common Name: **Star of Bethlehem, Chincherinchee, Chins**

Availability:	All year round.
Vase Life:	Approx 14–21 days.
Flower Notes:	Pronounced 'Or-ni-THOG-a-lum' this sturdy perennial flowering bulb produces clusters of star-shaped flowers on leafless stems. Some varieties have a bead-like black centre. Medium stem length.
Colour Range:	White, lemon, bright yellow, orange.

Ornithogalum thyrsoides

For the Florist:

- Ideal temperature range 8–10°C (46–50°F).
- Change water every 3–4 days, and avoid standing flowers in draughts or temperature fluctuations.
- Allow flowers to 'drink' for at least two hours before using in arrangements.
- Very sensitive to ethylene gas, display in a cool spot away from direct heat sources.
- Stem Type: Soft.
- Form: Line.

 Ornithogalum arabicum

For the Home:

- Re-cut stems and stand in clean, fresh water with flower food.
- Ornithogalum have an impressive vase life, to maximise this change water every 3–4 days, re-cutting stems each time.
- They are phototropic flowers, so expect them to follow light around the room.
- Very effective when arranged with bold foliages and flowers such as pink Nerines or white lilies.

For Weddings:
An individual flower which can be used successfully in traditional wedding designs, whilst still being a definite candidate for a bride looking for something more unusual. They can be arranged in both floral foam and vases. Individual flower heads will add an interesting bead-like texture to wired work. **Flower meaning:** Reconciliation.

For Students:
Family: Asparagaceae.
Genus: Ornithogalum.
Origin: South Africa, Mediterranean.
Flower Trivia: The slightly bizarre and almost unpronounceable common name of 'chincherinchee' is an anglicised version of 'tjenkenrientjee' the Afrikaans name for the flower.

Oxypetalum

Common Name: **Blue Tweedia, Southern star**

Availability: June — September.

Vase Life: Approx 14 — 21 days.

Flower Notes: Pronounced 'OXY-pet-a-lum' A scrambling, evergreen perennial with grey-green downy foliage and attractive flowers which develop into boat-shaped seed heads. Medium stem length.

Colour Range: Sky blue.

For the Florist:

- Ideal temperature range 2–5°C (36–41°F).
- Stems are latex producing, wash hands and tools after handling.
- Cut carefully with a sharp knife or scissors, taking care that the latex doesn't mark the foliage.
- Change water every other day and remove all foliage below water level.
- **Form:** Transitional.

For the Home:

- Re-cut stems and stand in clean, fresh water which should be changed every other day.
- Display at room temperature but away from direct heat.
- Wash hands thoroughly after handling, use gloves if allergic to latex.
- Flowers will continue to open after cutting and will mature to a deep lilac colour.
- Arrange with *Ammi visnaga* and Bouvardia in a tall vase for a summery display.

For Weddings:
A true blue flower with attractive foliage, Tweedia is perfect for informal summer weddings whether displayed in vases or designs in floral foam. It is latex producing which can be an irritant, so use in hand tied posies with care. This feature also makes it unsuitable for wiring although individual heads can be detached and cold glued for modern bridal work.

 Oxypetalum coeruleum
Syn: *Tweedia caerulea*

For Students:
Family: Apocynaceae.
Genus: Oxypetalum.
Native to: South America.
Flower Trivia: Loved by hummingbirds and butterflies, Oxypetalum is ideal for a wildlife friendly garden.

Paeonia

Common Name: **Peony**

Availability: February–July, peaks April–June.

Vase Life: Approx 5–10 days; five days in bud, up to five in flower.

Flower Notes: The large, luxurious taffeta-like flower head of the peony is unmistakable. It's easy to see why this flower is so popular with gardeners, florists and flower lovers alike. Medium stem length.

Colour Range: White, cream, lemon, peach, apricot, rose pink, deep pink, crimson, burgundy.

For the Florist:

- Ideal temperature range 8–12°C (46–54°F).
- Remove all leaves in contact with water and change water every 2–3 days.
- To encourage peonies to open, hold them upside down and spray with water to remove the sticky sap around the bud.
- To discourage them from opening too quickly, store in water in a cool, dark spot.
- Form: Round.

Paeonia 'Red Charm'

For the Home:

- Re-cut stems and stand in clean, fresh water with flower food.
- Change water every 2–3 days re-cutting stems every time. They are thirsty flowers, so check vase levels regularly.
- Stand in a cool spot to prolong vase life.
- Peonies prefer to be placed directly in water; they will wilt quickly if arranged in floral foam.
- They are beautiful arranged simply on their own, although a vase filled with stocks and peonies would look, and smell, fantastic.

For Weddings:
Its similarity to a rose in full bloom makes the peony a much sort after wedding flower. Wonderful in tied posies and vase designs, where it will add more than a touch of stately home elegance. Beware of its relatively short availability period, order well in advance to give them time to open.
Flower meaning: Bashfulness.

For Students:
Family: Paeoniaceae.
Genus: Paeonia.
Origin: Asia/S.Europe/N.America.
Flower Trivia: The Chinese city of Louyang is passionate about its peony, cultivating over 500,000 shrubs. It holds an annual peony festival in April.

Papaver

Common Name: **Iceland/Oriental poppy**

Availability: April–June as a cut flower. May–October as a seed head.

Vase Life: Approx 5–7 days.

Flower Notes: A cheerful, early summer flower with a distinctive seed head popular in dried arrangements. Medium stem length.

Colour Range: White, pink, red, orange, yellow, salmon.

For the Florist:

- Ideal temperature range 2–5°C (36–41°F).
- The stems produce latex which can be both a skin irritant and toxic to other flowers.
- To dilute the effects of the latex, stand the flowers alone in water for 24 hours after cutting.
- Poppies prefer shallow water which should be changed daily. Flower food is recommended.
- Keep out of draughts and direct heat sources.
- **Stem Type:** Soft.

For the Home:

- Re-cut stems and stand in clean, fresh, shallow water with flower food.
- Change water daily to minimise the effects of the latex which can cause the flower to wilt prematurely.
- Stand in a cool spot with good air circulation and out of direct heat.
- Always wash hands after use.
- Arrange in simple containers with other 'wild flowers' such as Tanacetum or *Ammi visnaga*.

 Papaver nudiflora 'Champagne Bubbles'

For Weddings:
The poppy's use in wedding work is limited – they don't last well in floral foam, and can be a skin irritant, so not ideal for tied posies either! They will look very effective when arranged in vases with similar wild meadow type flowers and ornamental grasses.
Flower meaning: Remembrance.

For Students:
Family: Papaveraceae.
Genus: Papaver.
Origin: Central Asia.
Flower Trivia: Universal symbols of remembrance, poppies were the only wild flowers which flourished on the battlefields of France in WW1.

Paphiopedilum

Common Name: **Slipper orchid, Venus slipper orchid**

Availability: November–April.

Vase Life: Approx 14–21 days.

Flower Notes: Pronounced 'Path-e-o-PED-e-lum' this is an unusual orchid with exotic striped and spotted markings and a large, bulbous lower lip. Short stem length.

Colour Range: White with pale green and tan markings.

For the Florist:

- Ideal temperature range 8–10°C (46–50°F).
- Stand in shallow water as hairs on the stem can contaminate water.
- Change water every 4–5 days and display away from direct heat sources and draughts.
- Mist regularly; high humidity is important to ensure maximum vase life.

For the Home:

- Re-cut stems and stand in clean, fresh, shallow water.
- Change water every 4–5 days, there is no need to add flower food.
- Central heating will dehydrate the flower. Display away from radiators in a draught free spot and mist daily.
- Arrange in a bud vase with loops of grass or rolled leaves for something a little more unusual.

Paphiopedilum leeanum

For Weddings:
It would be a shame to use this flower in informal tieds; it really needs to be shown off in more modern, European-style designs. Add it into structured bridal bouquets with Phalaenopsis or Vanda orchids with a burnt orange, cream and lime colour scheme. They would make unusual buttonholes.

For Students:
Family: Orchidaceae.

Genus: Paphiopedilum.

Origin: Far East.

Flower Trivia: New varieties are still being discovered. *P. armeniacum* 'Golden slipper orchid' was found in Yunnan province in China in 1979.

Phalaenopsis

Common Name: **Moth orchid**

Availability: All year round.

Vase Life: Approx 7–14 days.

Flower Notes: Extremely popular as a pot plant, Phalaenopsis are also tremendous cut flowers, adding instant sophistication to designs. Many of them have distinctive markings with contrasting coloured throats. Long stem length.

Colour Range: Pure white, cream, lemon, pale pink, lilac, cerise pink, eggshell green.

For the Florist:

- Ideal temperature range 7–15°C (44–59°F).
- Lower temperatures may cause flowers to blacken.
- A humid atmosphere is important, mist frequently and keep out of draughts.
- Wilting flowers can be revived by floating them on water at room temperature for 15–30 minutes.
- These flowers are very sensitive to ethylene gas.
- **Form:** Line/Transitional.

Phalaenopsis 'Shanghai'

For the Home:

- Re-cut stems at an angle and stand in clean, fresh water with flower food.
- Phalaenopsis are happy in warm rooms, but should be out of draughts and direct heat.
- For maximum vase life, mist lightly every day.

For Weddings:
An elegant and distinctive choice, equally happy in structured designs, particularly in limited shower bouquets, or cascading from lush and extravagant arrangements. Individual heads are robust enough to be wired and glued.
Flower Meaning: Love, beauty and refinement.

For Students:
Family: Orchidaceae.
Genus: Phalaenopsis.
Origin: Tropical Asia.
Flower Trivia: There are over 50 species of Phalaenopsis; the genus was first established in 1825 by the Dutch botanist C. L Blume.

Phlox

Common Name: **Phlox**

Availability: All year round.

Vase Life: Approx 7–14 days.

Flower Notes: Pronounced 'flocks', this fragrant flower is a popular perennial and a cottage garden favourite. The almost flat flowers form in clusters with an attractive deeper coloured centre. Medium stem length.

Colour Range: Pure white, cream, pale pink, deep pink, mauve, purple.

For the Florist:

- Ideal temperature range 8–10°C (46–50°F).
- Remove all leaves in contact with water and use flower food.
- Change water every 4–5 days and keep out of direct heat sources.
- Very sensitive to ethylene gas.
- Wilting flowers can be revived by re-cutting stems and standing in a cooler for 2–3 hours.
- **Form:** Transitional.

For the Home:

- Re-cut stems and stand in clean, fresh water which should be changed every 4–5 days.
- Remove all foliage in contact with water.
- Phlox are thirsty flowers, so check vase levels daily; flower food is recommended.
- Stand in a cool spot with good air circulation.
- Phlox will look gorgeous arranged on their own or add roses and Delphiniums for a summery display.

 Phlox paniculata 'Bright Eyes'

For Weddings:
A very pretty, fragrant flower available in a range of subtle hues which makes it very popular for weddings. Although sometimes a little too bushy for tied designs, Phlox can be cut down and used in table arrangements, or left long stemmed for vases and pedestals.
Flower meaning: Our souls are united.

For Students:
Family: Polemoniaceae.
Genus: Phlox.
Origin: North America.
Flower Trivia: Phlox was introduced into England from the USA in the 1700's by plant explorer John Bartram, considered to be the father of American botany.

134

Physalis

Common Name: **Chinese lantern, Bladder cherry**

Availability: July–November, peaks August–October.

Vase Life: Approx 6–10 days.

Flower Notes: Pronounced 'Fe-SAL-is'. Physalis has mid-green heart-shaped leaves with a lantern-like calyx surrounding an orange, cherry-sized fruit. It is grown primarily for its vivid autumn colours. Medium stem length.

Colour Range: Bright orange.

For the Florist:

- Ideal temperature range 2–5°C (36–41°F).
- Remove all leaves in contact with water and change water every 2–3 days.
- If preferred, the leaves can be removed to show off the orange lanterns.
- Handle with care as the delicate outer calyx is easily crushed.
- **Form:** Line.

For the Home:

- Re-cut stems and stand in clean, fresh water.
- Change water every 2–3 days, flower food is not necessary.
- Although it is used in herbal medicine, eating Physalis which has been commercially grown for the cut flower market is not recommended.
- To dry Physalis, remove leaves and air dry by hanging upside down in a cool spot. Alternatively, carefully pick off the lanterns and dry by spreading them out on a flat dish.

 Physalis alkekengi 'Lampions'

For Weddings:
Stems of Physalis would be very distinctive in large arrangements or tall vase designs. The individual 'lanterns' could be scattered on tables with crab apples and red oak leaves to create a real seasonal feel to an autumn wedding. Great for Halloween as well!

For Students:
Family: Asparagaceae.

Genus: Physalis.

Origin: Europe, Asia, Japan.

Flower Trivia: The fruit, a tiny orange berry inside the calyx, is used in homeopathy to treat bladder and kidney disorders.

Physostegia

Common Name: **Obedient plant, False dragonhead**

Availability: July–September.

Vase Life: Approx 7–14 days.

Flower Notes: Pronounced 'Fi-SOS-tea-gia'. A pretty perennial with spikes of attractive, tube-shaped flowers that resemble mini snapdragons. It has an unusual square stem which gives it a very uniform and neat appearance. Medium stem length.

Colour Range: White, pink, mauve.

🌸 *Physostegia virginiana*

For the Florist:

- Ideal temperature range 2–5°C (36–41°F).
- Remove all leaves in contact with water.
- Change water every 4–5 days, flower food is recommended.
- Keep out of the sun and direct heat sources.
- **Form:** Line.

For the Home:

- Re-cut stems and stand in clean, fresh water.
- Add flower food and change vase water every 4–5 days.
- To prolong vase life, stand in a cool spot out of direct sunlight.
- Arrange with large-headed flowers such as roses, sunflowers or carnations.

For Weddings:

A little too rigid for shower bouquets, Physostegia's delicate flowers, which open from the bottom up, would be lost in all but the loosest of tied posies. Arrange instead in vases and reception designs to show off its 'just picked' look. It would coordinate well in a pink/purple colour scheme.

For Students:

Family: Lamiaceae.

Genus: Physostegia.

Origin: Eastern USA.

Flower Trivia: Known as obedient plant or accommodation flower because individual flower heads can be rotated to any angle and once moved, will stay in that position.

Polianthes

Common Name: **Tuberose**

Availability: December–July.

Vase Life: Approx 7–10 days.

Flower Notes: Pronounced 'Poll-lee-AN-thees'. A tuberous plant with waxy, highly fragrant, star-shaped flowers clustered tightly together on a slim spike. Its sweet scent is used extensively in the perfume industry. Tall stem length.

Colour Range: Creamy white with pink tips.

For the Florist:

- Ideal temperature range 8–15°C (46–59°F).
- Prolonged exposure to cold will reduce its fragrance.
- Lower temperatures can prevent the flowers from opening.
- Tuberose will grow towards the light, pinch out the tips to help to keep flowers straight.
- **Form:** Line.

For the Home:

- Re-cut stems and stand in clean, fresh water.
- Flower food is recommended to encourage buds to open and to preserve its perfume.
- Nip off the lower buds as they die as they produce ethylene gas which can shorten the flower's vase life.
- Arrange in tall vases with large-headed roses, Delphiniums or peonies for a fragrant summery display.

 Polianthes tuberosa

For Weddings:
Use the highly scented flowers of tuberose in large, showy designs or more limited arrangements – they will adapt to either style. The individual florets can be added into wired work, but hay fever sufferers may find their strong scent overpowering.
Flower meaning: Illicit pleasures.

For Students:
Family: Agavaceae.
Genus: Polianthes.
Origin: Mexico.
Flower Trivia: The Aztecs called the night flowering tuberose 'Omixochitl' meaning bone flower, due to the almost luminous qualities of its white flowers.

Polygonatum

Common Name: **Solomon's seal**

Availability: February–June, peaks March–May.

Vase Life: Approx 5–7 days.

Flower Notes: Pronounced 'Poll-lee-go-NA-tum'. A pretty herbaceous perennial usually found growing in shady areas. It has graceful arching stems supporting pairs of delicate, bell-like flowers. Medium stem length.

Colour Range: White with pale green tips.

For the Florist:

- Ideal temperature range 2–5°C (36–41°F).
- Cut approx 2cm (1") from stems and place immediately in water with flower food.
- Handle with care as the arching stems can tangle easily.
- Mist occasionally to keep up humidity.
- To prevent flowers from drying out display away from draughts and heat sources.
- **Stem Type:** Soft.
- **Form:** Line.

For the Home:

- Re-cut stems and place in clean water.
- Flower food is recommended.
- Keep out of direct heat sources, they prefer cooler conditions.
- Change water every 2–3 days and mist occasionally.
- Bring a taste of early summer into the house by combining Polygonatum with blue Agapanthus and pale pink roses.

 Polygonatum multiflorum

For Weddings:
A very pretty, delicate flower that needs space in an arrangement for it to be appreciated. Use in designs where graceful, soft outlines are needed, remove the leaves for greater form and definition. The long line of flowers running down the stem makes it tricky to use in tied posies and it is a little too soft for wired work.

For Students:
Family: Asparagaceae.
Genus: Polygonatum.
Origin: Northern hemisphere.
Flower Trivia: Solomon's seal has been used in herbal medicine for thousands of years, and was often used as a poultice to prevent excessive bleeding.

Protea

Common Name: **Honey pot, Sugar bush**

Availability: All year round, with different varieties peaking within that time.

Vase Life: Can be kept for up to a month.

Flower Notes: A fascinating tropical flower of waxy, scale-like bracts which form a 'cup' around the soft fluffy flowers massed inside. There is a huge variety of shapes within the genus. Short to medium stem length.

Colour Range: Creamy white, fiery orange, rich maroon/brown, silvery pink, sage green.

For the Florist:

- Ideal temperature range 5–10°C (41–50°F).
- Blackening of the flower head is a common problem, to prevent this, avoid storing Protea in the dark.
- Good air circulation is important to stop mould forming in the centre of the flower head.
- Remove all leaves in contact with water and change water every other day.
- Flower food is recommended.
- **Stem Type:** Woody.
- **Form:** Round.

 Protea neriifolia x susannae 'Pink Ice'

For the Home:

- Re-cut stems with secateurs and stand in clean, fresh water, avoiding chlorinated water if possible.
- Protea are thirsty flowers so check water levels daily. Flower food is recommended.
- Protea generate a lot of heat, so to prolong vase life display in a cool spot.
- Dry Protea by hanging them upside down in a cool, dry, airy place. Their colour will fade with age.
- For texture and richness arrange with Leucospernum, Celosia or Banksia.

For Weddings:
Not automatically associated with wedding work, although a flower bouquet made entirely of these fascinating flowers would be an absolute show stopper. Use them to add visual weight and texture to vase designs and arrangements, in particular for autumn and winter weddings. Individual bracts can be wired into boutonnières and corsages.

For Students:
Family: Proteaceae.
Genus: Protea.
Origin: South Africa.
Flower Trivia: The Proteaceae family is an ancient one, dating back some 300 million years. Modern day proteas were discovered by botanists in the 1600's and introduced into Britain in the 1700's.

139

Ranunculus

Common Name: **Turban/Persian buttercup**

Availability:	October–June, peaks December–May.
Vase Life:	Approx 7–10 days.
Flower Notes:	One of the loveliest of spring flowers with richly coloured paper-thin petals packed tightly together resembling an almost perfect rosette. Short stem length.
Colour Range:	Lustrous tones of white, lemon, yellow, orange, peach, gold, pale & dark pink, red, burgundy.

For the Florist:

- Ideal temperature range 2–10°C (36–50°F).
- Can be a water polluter, change vase water every 1–2 days and use flower food.
- Keep wrapped in paper while conditioning to stop the stems from curving.
- Do not mist, as this can encourage fungal growth.
- **Stem Type:** Hollow.
- **Form:** Round.

For the Home:

- Re-cut stems at an angle with scissors and place in clean, fresh water.
- They can become top heavy when open. A wire inserted carefully inside the stem will help to support the flower.
- Stand in a cool position and be prepared for the flowers to curve naturally towards the light.
- Change water every other day and use flower food.
- Celebrate the spring by filling vases with Ranunculus, tulips, hellebores and Genista.

 Ranunculus asiaticus 'Elegance Red'

For Weddings:
Perfect for the spring bride, the delicate, papery flowers of Ranunculus look fabulous in tied posies. Its wide range of colours enables it to fit in with any scheme, although its soft stem makes it unsuitable for buttonholes and for arranging in floral foam.
Flower Meaning: I am dazzled by your charms.

For Students:
Family: Ranunculaceae.
Genus: Ranunculus.
Origin: S/W Asia & Europe.
Flower Trivia: A member of the buttercup family; its name is a derivative of the Latin word for 'frog' referring to the swampy places where the flowers are often found.

Rosa

Common Name: **Rose**

Availability: All year round.

Vase Life: Approx 7–14 days.

Flower Notes: The world's favourite flower! Fragrant and with a huge range of colours and varieties from big showy hybrid teas to delicate miniatures, the appeal of the rose is easy to understand. Medium/tall stem length.

Colour Range: All colours and shades including green – although no true black or blue rose.

For the Florist:

- Ideal temperature range 2–5°C (36–41°F). Warmer temperatures can shorten vase life.

Rosa 'Darcey' (David Austin)

- Roses are very sensitive to bacteria, so it's important that all vases and containers are clean.
- Remove all leaves below the water line and only remove thorns where necessary. Don't use a rose stripper as this can damage the stem.
- Stand in a cool spot in cold water which should be changed every 2–3 days, and add flower food.
- **Stem Type:** Woody.
- **Form:** Round.

For the Home:

- Re-cut stems at an angle, preferably with a knife, and stand in fresh, cold water in a clean vase.
- Use flower food and change water every 2–3 days. Remove all foliage in contact with water.
- Display your roses at home in a cool spot, out of direct sunlight and heat sources.
- To dry roses; remove foliage, arrange in a fan shape and secure with a rubber band. Hang upside down in a cool, airy place for 2–3 weeks.

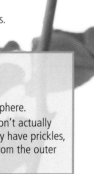

For Weddings:
A rose has everything; style, elegance and fragrance – although not all commercially grown varieties are scented. Whether as a simple, single buttonhole or part of an elaborate bouquet, the rose is an enduring and deservedly popular choice for wedding flowers.
Flower Meaning: Love.

For Students:
Family: Rosaceae.
Genus: Rosa.
Origin: Northern hemisphere.
Flower Trivia: Roses don't actually have thorns; instead they have prickles, sharp growths formed from the outer layers of the stem.

Rosa (Spray)

Common Name: **Spray rose**

Availability: All year round.

Vase Life: Approx 7–12 days.

Flower Notes: A pretty delicate rose with anywhere between 3–11 heads on a single stem. With smaller flowers than the single headed rose they have a charming, porcelain delicacy about them. Medium stem length.

Colour Range: In all colours and shades with the exception of green, blue and black.

For the Florist:

- Ideal temperature range 2–5°C (36–41°F).
- Roses are very sensitive to bacteria, so it's important that all vases and containers are clean.
- Remove all leaves in contact with water but only remove thorns if necessary.
- Change water every 2–3 days and use flower food.
- Display in a cool spot with good air circulation to minimise the effects of ethylene gas and botrytis.
- **Stem Type:** Woody.
- **Form:** Transitional.

For the Home:

- Re-cut stems and stand in fresh, cold water in a clean vase.
- Add flower food change water every 2–3 days.
- Stand in a cool spot with good air circulation. Remove any leaves in contact with water.
- Arrange spray roses with Veronica, larkspur or sweet peas for a natural, country look.

 Rosa 'Tiramisu'

For Weddings:
Spray roses are perfect for softening the line of shower bouquets and tied posies, where a very natural, understated look is required. They are also the ideal size and weight for wiring into corsages, buttonholes, hair flowers and cake decorations
Flower Meaning: Grace.

For Students:
Family: Rosaceae.
Genus: Rosa.
Origin: Northern Europe.
Flower Trivia: Floribunda is a relatively modern rose originally produced by crossing a hybrid tea with a polyantha rose. Many, but not all are fragrant.

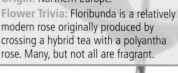

Rudbeckia

Common Name: **Black-eyed Susan, Orange coneflower**

Availability: July–September.

Vase Life: Approx 6–8 days.

Flower Notes: A cheerful perennial, beloved by gardeners and very popular in herbaceous borders. Most commonly sold commercially as a spiky seed head. Medium stem length.

Colour Range: Seed head; chestnut brown, flower; yellow/burgundy.

For the Florist:

- Ideal temperature range 2–5°C (36–41°F).
- If stems are limp, revive by re-cutting before wrapping in paper and standing in deep water.
- Keep out of the sun and direct heat sources as this will dry out the flower prematurely.
- **Form:** Round.

For the Home:

- Re-cut stems and stand in clean, fresh water.
- Flower food is recommended, and water should be changed every 2–3 days.
- The showy centres of Rudbeckia are suitable for drying, simply hang upside down in bunches in a cool spot with good air circulation.
- Use to add texture to vases of tall gladioli, sunflowers and Crocosmia.

Rudbeckia sp.

For Students:

Family: Asteraceae.

Genus: Rudbeckia.

Origin: North America.

Flower Trivia: Professor Olof Rudbeck was the botany teacher of Carolus Linnaeus 'The Father of Modern Taxonomy' who named the flower in honour of his mentor.

Salvia

Common Name: **Sage**

Availability: April–October, peaks April–June.

Vase Life: Approx 6–8 days.

Flower Notes: A popular culinary herb, Salvia also makes a great cut flower with neat, slim delicate spikes and attractive aromatic foliage. Medium stem length.

Colour Range: Violet blue.

For the Florist:

- Ideal temperature range 2–8°C (36–46°F).
- Remove all leaves in contact with water and add flower food.
- Change water every 2–3 days, re-cutting stems each time. Don't overcrowd vases.
- Keep out of sun and direct heat sources.
- **Form:** Line.

For the Home:

- Re-cut stems and stand in clean, fresh water with flower food.
- To prolong vase life, stand in a cool spot out of direct sunlight, changing water every 2–3 days.
- Commercially grown Salvia may have been treated with chemicals - be wary of using it in the kitchen.
- Dry Salvia by suspending in small bunches in a dark, dry location. Drying should take between 2–3 weeks.
- The slim lines of Salvia would look lovely arranged with pink peonies and scabious.

Salvia pratensis 'Rhapsody in Blue'

For Weddings:
For any bride who is looking for a natural, country style, Salvia is a must. Its strong violet colour contrasts beautifully with pinks and purples, it would add movement and line to tied posies not forgetting a touch of vintage chic to vase and table designs. Can also be used in wired work.
Flower meaning: Wisdom.

For Students:
Family: Lamiaceae.
Genus: Salvia.
Origin: Central Europe/Western Asia.
Flower Trivia: Easy to grow in the garden, plant Salvia in your vegetable patch to repel carrot fly and cabbage worm. Meadow sage tea is believed to fortify the body and prevent apoplexy.

Sandersonia

Common Name: **Christmas bells, Chinese lantern lily**

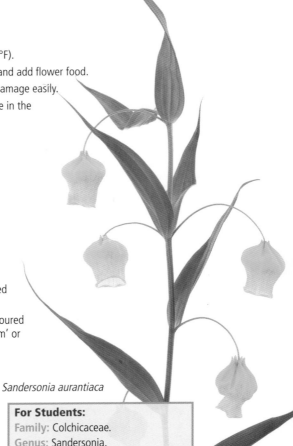

Availability: All year round.

Vase Life: Approx 14–21 days.

Flower Notes: The distinctive, lantern-like flowers of Sandersonia were once a common sight in the grasslands of South Africa. Due to intensive farming it is now mostly confined to nature reserves. Medium stem length.

Colour Range: Pale orange, yellow.

For the Florist:

- Ideal temperature range 5–10°C (41–50°F).
- Remove all leaves in contact with water and add flower food.
- Handle carefully as the delicate flowers damage easily.
- Sandersonia needs plenty of light; storage in the dark will shorten its vase life.
- **Stem Type:** Soft.
- **Form:** Line/Transitional.

For the Home:

- Re-cut stems and stand in clean, fresh water with flower food.
- Display in a warm, light position for maximum vase life and change water every 3–4 days.
- Sandersonia will last equally well arranged in water or in floral foam.
- Arrange in a tall vase with fresh, lime coloured flowers such as *Viburnum opulus* 'Roseum' or shamrock Chrysanthemum blooms.

 Sandersonia aurantiaca

For Weddings:

Despite its delicate appearance, Sandersonia is a reliable flower for large pedestal and function designs. It will look particularly effective with tall flowers such as gladioli and lilies. Although available all year, its colour lends itself to an autumnal theme.

For Students:

Family: Colchicaceae.

Genus: Sandersonia.

Origin: South Africa.

Flower Trivia: Flower growers in New Zealand were first to produce Sandersonia as a successful cut flower. It is a constant best seller 'down under'.

145

Scabiosa

Common Name: **Scabious, Pincushion flower**

Availability: May–November, peaks June–October.

Vase Life: Approx 6–8 days.

Flower Notes: Pronounced 'Sca-BOW-sia'. A popular cottage garden plant with delicate papery petals surrounding a hard 'pincushion' centre. Medium stem length.

Colour Range: Creamy white, pale lilac, sky blue, deep burgundy/brown.

For the Florist:

- Ideal temperature range 2–5°C (36–41°F).
- Remove all leaves in contact with water and add flower food.
- Change water every 2–3 days, re-cutting stems each time to keep a flow of fresh water to the flower head.
- Petal drop can be due to exposure to ethylene gas. Display away from possible sources in a well-ventilated spot.
- **Form:** Round.

Scabiosa stellata

For the Home:

- Re-cut stems and stand in clean, fresh water which should be changed every 2–3 days.
- Scabious is a water polluter so always use flower food and make sure vases are clean.
- Stand in a cool spot with good air circulation and out of direct heat sources.
- Suitable for drying – hang flowers upside down in small bunches in a cool area with ventilation. They should take about two weeks to dry.
- Scabious will look gorgeous mixed with summer flowers such as Nigella, larkspur and Tanacetum.

 Scabiosa caucasica 'Staefa'

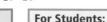

For Weddings:

A perfect flower for a summer bride looking for soft pastel shades. Arrange with either creamy whites or greens or add to pink tones for a gentle contrast. Add carefully into tied posies and simple vase designs so that the delicate flowers are not overwhelmed. The dried seed head can be used in wired work.

For Students:

Family: Caprifoliaceae.

Genus: Scabiosa.

Origin: Mediterranean.

Flower Trivia: Scabiosa comes from the Latin word for itch; herbalists used the flower to treat a range of skin conditions which included removing unwanted freckles.

Scilla

Common Name: **Squill**

Availability: March and April.

Vase Life: Approx 7–10 days.

Flower Notes: Pronounced 'Cilla'. A spring flowering bulb whose wild counterpart the bluebell is famous for carpets of deep blue formed in woodlands in late spring. Short stem length.

Colour Range: Pale blue, white.

For the Florist:

- Ideal temperature range 5–10°C (41–50°F).
- Storing in lower temperatures can damage the flowers.
- If Scilla arrives 'dry', condition at room temperature for at least two hours before using.
- Never leave out of water as the flower dries out very easily.
- **Stem Type:** Soft.
- **Form:** Line.

For the Home:

- Re-cut stems and stand in clean, fresh water.
- Change water every 2–3 days, re-cutting stems each time.
- Stand in a warm spot, but out of draughts and direct heat.
- Arrange with yellow Ranunculus and 'Paper White' Narcissi for a refreshing spring combination.

 Scilla sp.

For Weddings:

A gorgeous late spring flower, very similar to a wild bluebell which makes it perfect for brides searching for a typical English seasonal flower. Mix with lemons and creams or pale pinks in simple tied posies, or arrange casually in china vases for that classic vintage look.

Flower meaning: Constancy.

For Students:

Family: Asparagaceae.

Genus: Scilla.

Origin: Europe & Asia.

Flower Trivia: If you want to have bluebells in your home, then commercially grown Scilla is an excellent alternative to the wild bluebell, which is protected under the Wildlife and Countryside Act.

Sedum

Common Name: **Showy stonecrop, Ice plant**

Availability: June–November, peaks July–October.

Vase Life: Approx 6–8 days.

Flower Notes: A popular garden succulent with thick, fleshy leaves and flat flower heads composed of dozens of tiny star-shaped flowers. Medium stem length.

Colour Range: Sage green maturing to pink then ruby red.

For the Florist:

- Ideal temperature range 5–8°C (41–46°F).
- Remove any leaves in contact with water.
- Change water every 2–3 days and add flower food.
- Keep out of the sun and direct heat sources. A cool position will prolong vase life.
- **Form:** Transitional.

For the Home:

- Re-cut stems and stand in clean, fresh water.
- Remove foliage touching or below the water line.
- Flower food is recommended, and water should be changed every 2–3 days.
- Stand in a cool spot with good air circulation.
- Emphasise Sedum's texture by combining it with berried ivy, Amaranthus and Celosia. Suitable for using in floral foam.

 *Sedum spectabile* 'Autumn Joy'

For Weddings:

Sedum is lovely for autumn weddings; add into informal tied posy designs and simple vases. If the flower heads are too solid, save them for using in larger venue arrangements. Sedum's tight green flowers develop into a rich fluffy pink as they mature. Suitable for using in wiring work.

Flower meaning: Tranquillity.

For Students:

Family: Crassulaceae.

Genus: Hylotelephium.

Origin: Eastern Asia.

Flower Trivia: Commonly called Ice plant because the dense flower head retains sparkling droplets of rain. The Sedum genus is synonymous with Hylotelephium.

Skimmia

Availability: September–June, peaks September–March.

Vase Life: Approx 10–14 days.

Flower Notes: An aromatic evergreen shrub with shapely dark green leaves and clusters of tight flower buds which open up into tiny, highly scented flowers in the early spring. Short stem length.

Colour Range: Ruby red buds followed by white flowers.

For the Florist:

- Ideal temperature range 2–10°C (36–50°F).
- Temperatures lower than 2°C (36°F) can turn the foliage black.
- Remove all leaves in contact with water.
- Change water every 3–4 days using flower food specifically for shrubs if possible.
- **Stem Type:** Woody.
- **Form:** Transitional.

For the Home:

- Re-cut stems with secateurs and stand in clean, fresh water.
- Use flower food and change water every 3–4 days, re-cutting stems each time.
- Stand in a warm spot but away from direct heat.
- Use Skimmia to add texture to arrangements in floral foam. Group in vases with hellebores and white hyacinths at Christmas time.

 Skimmia japonica 'Rubella'

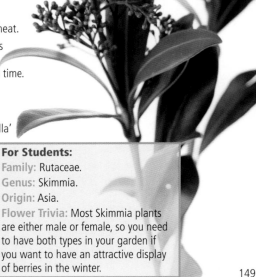

For Weddings:

The deep green and red of Skimmia really does lend itself to a Christmas wedding. A very dependable flower for arrangements or vases, it would also look very pretty in small tied posies, especially when mixed with berries and other textural flowers. Excellent for wiring into buttonholes and corsages.

For Students:

Family: Rutaceae.

Genus: Skimmia.

Origin: Asia.

Flower Trivia: Most Skimmia plants are either male or female, so you need to have both types in your garden if you want to have an attractive display of berries in the winter.

149

Solidago

Common Name: **Golden rod, Soli**

Availability: All year round.

Vase Life: Approx 8–12 days.

Flower Notes: Commonly seen growing vigorously on waste land, commercially grown Solidago - although perhaps not the most attractive of flowers - is good value for money and very versatile. Tall stem length.

Colour Range: Mustard, bright yellow.

For the Florist:

- Ideal temperature range 2–5°C (36–41°F).
- Strip off all leaves in contact with water.
- The stems can easily clog up with bacteria, re-cut them every 2–3 days changing the water each time.
- Ensure all buckets and containers are clean and use flower food.
- **Form:** Filler.

For the Home:

- Re-cut stems and stand in clean, fresh water with flower food.
- Re-cut stems and change water every 2–3 days.
- Dry Solidago by tying into small bunches and hanging upside down in a cool place.
- Solidago can be used to fill out vases of large-headed flowers; it also lasts well in floral foam.

 Solidago 'Knock Out'

For Students:

Family: Asteraceae.

Genus: Solidago.

Origin: North America.

Flower Trivia: Almost indistinguishable from Solidago is solidaster, a cross between Solidago and Aster which was developed in Lyons in 1909.

Spathiphyllum

Common Name: **Peace lily, Spathe flower**

Availability: All year round.

Vase Life: Approx 7–14 days.

Flower Notes: Pronounced 'Spath-e-FIL-lum'. More commonly recognised as a houseplant, Spathiphyllum as a cut flower is relatively new. They are similar in appearance to a small Anthurium. Medium stem length.

Colour Range: Pure white.

For the Florist:

- Ideal temperature range 8–18°C (46–64°F).
- Temperatures below 8°C (46°F) can cause the flowers to blacken.
- Keep out of draughts and excess heat sources as this can cause the flower to wilt.
- Re-hydrate limp flowers by misting or submerging in lukewarm water for a few minutes.
- They are delicate flowers, so handle with care.
- **Stem Type:** Soft.
- **Form:** Line.

For the Home:

- Re-cut stems and stand in clean, fresh water.
- Use flower food and change the water every 3–4 days.
- Stand in a warm spot, but out of direct heat and sunlight.
- Arrange Spathiphyllum in groups for more impact; they last well in floral foam or in vases.

 Spathiphyllum wallisii 'X-ray'

For Weddings:
The small and delicate Spathiphyllum works surprisingly well in wedding designs. It is at home with traditional flowers such as roses and also more tropical varieties where it can take the place of Anthuriums or Zantedeschia. Ideal for a more contemporary style of bouquet, it can also be wired into buttonholes and corsages.

For Students:
Family: Araceae.

Genus: Spathiphyllum.

Origin: Tropical Americas, Asia.

Flower Trivia: Spathiphyllum plants are a natural air freshener, absorbing hazardous substances from the air and replacing them with pure oxygen. They are in NASA's top ten of air purifying plants.

Spiraea

Common Name: **Spirea, Bridal wreath**

Availability: January–October, with different varieties peaking within that period.

Vase Life: Approx 6–8 days.

Flower Notes: Pronounced 'Spy-REAR'. A popular deciduous fast growing shrub which naturalises and spreads easily in the garden. Flowers prolifically in late spring and summer. Medium stem length.

Colour Range: Pure white, candyfloss pink.

For the Florist:

- Ideal temperature range 2–5°C (36–41°F).
- Remove all leaves in contact with water.
- Change water every 2–3 days, re-cutting stems each time.
- Keep out of direct heat sources, as this will dry out the flower prematurely.
- **Stem Type:** Woody.
- **Form:** Line.

For the Home:

- Re-cut stems with secateurs and stand in clean, fresh water with flower food.
- Change the water every 2–3 days, re-cutting stems each time.
- If arranging in floral foam, make sure that the container is kept topped up with water.
- Arrange Spiraea in large vases with similar cottage garden flowers such as Delphiniums, lupins or peonies.

 Spiraea nipponica 'Snowmound'

For Weddings:
The garden style of Spiraea lends itself ideally to a country house reception. A little too stiff to add into formal bridal work although the arching stems of *Spiraea* 'Snowmound' would look rather lovely in natural tied posies. Use full length in large venue designs to create an impressive display.

For Students:
Family: Rosaceae.
Genus: Spiraea.
Origin: Northern hemisphere.
Flower Trivia: *Spiraea ulmaira* or Meadowsweet, is a very common wild flower which can be found growing in woodland, damp meadows and on river banks.

Stephanotis

Common Name: **Madagascar jasmine, Bridal veil vine**

Availability: June–December.

Vase Life: Approx 4–5 days.

Flower Notes: Pronounced 'Steph-an-OH-tis'. A hothouse vine of highly scented star-shaped flowers with a waxy appearance set against dark green shiny leaves. For floristry use, individual flower heads are sold in packs, rather than by the stem.

Colour Range: Pure white.

For the Florist:

- Ideal temperature range 2–5°C (36–41°F).
- Stephanotis flowers are sold in airtight containers which can be left unopened for up to 5 days in a cool spot with high humidity.
- Keep away from sources of ethylene gas.
- They require a humid atmosphere so once the container is opened spray the flowers lightly every day.
- Wilting flowers can be revived by submerging them briefly in tepid water.

For the Home:

- Keep the container airtight and unopened until you need to use the flowers.
- Once opened, spray gently to keep up humidity.
- An alternative to buying the flowers is to purchase a Stephanotis plant which should be kept in a warm room out of direct heat and draughts.
- Avoid moving or turning the plant as this can cause the flowers to drop off. Mist gently everyday.

 Stephanotis floribunda

For Weddings:
The scented Stephanotis is a traditional bridal flower that has a touch of old-fashioned glamour and style. Wire into formal shower bouquets, corsages and Alice bands or wear as individual flowers in the hair.
Flower meaning: Marital happiness.

For Students:
Family: Apocynaceae.
Genus: Stephanotis.
Origin: Madagascar.
Flower Trivia: Its name comes from the Ancient Greek 'stephanos' for crown and 'otis' for ear, a reference to the flower's ear-shaped stamens.

153

Strelitzia

Common Name: **Bird-of-paradise, Crane flower**

Availability: All year round.

Vase Life: Approx 12–18 days.

Flower Notes: An extremely popular tropical flower with brightly coloured petals forming a distinctive crest rising from a thick, fibrous stem. Tall stem length.

Colour Range: Vibrant orange and blue.

For the Florist:

- Ideal temperature range 10–15°C (50–59°F).
- Lower temperatures can cause the flowers to turn brown.
- Change water every other day, re-cutting stems each time to ensure a constant flow of water to the flower.
- Display out of draughts in a warm spot with good air circulation.
- **Form:** Line.

For the Home:

- Re-cut stems with secateurs and stand in a tall vase with clean, fresh water.
- For maximum vase life, change water every other day re-cutting stems each time.
- There is a second flower tucked inside the green pointed spathe; tease it out gently when the first flower starts to fade.
- The jelly like substance which oozes from the flower can be wiped off with a damp cloth.

 Strelitzia reginae

For Students:
Family: Strelitziaceae.
Genus: Strelitzia.
Origin: South Africa.
Flower Trivia: Despite Strelitzia's modern appearance, they were first introduced into Britain in 1773 by Sir Joseph Banks and exhibited at the Royal Botanic Gardens at Kew.

Symphoricarpos

Common Name: **Snowberry**

Availability: August–October.

Vase Life: Approx 7–14 days.

Flower Notes: Pronounced 'Sim-forrey-CAR-pus'. A member of the honeysuckle family, Symphoricarpos is a twiggy shrub with distinctive ornamental berries borne in tight clusters. Tall stem length.

Colour Range: White, lime, pale green, pale pink.

For the Florist:

- Ideal temperature range 6–8°C (43–46°F).
- Change water every 2–3 days, re-cutting stems each time.
- Keep out of direct heat sources, as this can cause the berries to fall.
- Misting gently every day will also help to prevent berry drop.
- **Stem Type:** Woody.
- **Form:** Line.

For the Home:

- Re-cut stems, preferably with secateurs and stand in clean, fresh water.
- Change water every 2–3 days and display in a cool spot out of direct heat.
- The gelatinous substance inside the berries can be an irritant, so always wash hands after use.
- Very effective when arranged with large-headed flowers such as Amaryllis or Chrysanthemum blooms.

 Symphoricarpos 'Sweet Fantasy'

For Weddings:

A lovely choice for an autumn wedding adding texture and a seasonal feel to tied posies, vase designs and large arrangements. If crushed, the berries ooze a jelly-like goo, which although won't permanently stain, will mark, so be wary of it near expensive dresses! Can be wired with care.

For Students:

Family: Caprifoliaceae.

Genus: Symphoricarpos.

Origin: North & Central America.

Flower Trivia: Common snowberry, which grows wild in many places, is an important food source in winter for birds such as pheasant and grouse.

Syringa

Common Name: **Lilac**

Availability:	October–June, peaks December–April.
Vase Life:	Approx 5–10 days.
Flower Notes:	Pronounced 'Sir-RIN-jar'. A deciduous spring flowering ornamental tree with heart-shaped leaves and clusters of small, highly fragrant flowers. Tall stem length.
Colour Range:	Pure white, pale lilac, deep lilac, pale pink.

For the Florist:

- Ideal temperature range 2–8°C (36–46°F).
- On first conditioning, wrap flower heads in paper to support them and place in deep water with shrub food overnight.
- Syringa is a thirsty flower – keep vases topped up. Re-cut stems daily.
- Very sensitive to ethylene gas.
- **Stem Type:** Woody.
- **Form:** Line.

For the Home:

- Re-cut stems with secateurs and stand in clean, fresh water with flower or shrub food.
- Change water every other day, re-cutting stems each time.
- Syringa does not last well in floral foam. If using in arrangements, keep the container topped up with water.
- For an impressive display, stand in tall vases with Moluccella and large-headed roses.

Syringa vulgaris 'Katherine Havemeyer'

For Weddings:
One of the few tall spring flowers, lilac can be added into large venue designs, or if needed, cut short for smaller work. Its frothy flowers and sweet scent will enhance bridesmaids' posies and bridal tieds, and its cottage garden appeal is perfect for 'vintage' styling. Unsuitable for wiring work.
Flower meaning: Beauty.

For Students:
Family: Oleaceae.
Genus: Syringa.
Origin: S/E Europe & Asia.
Flower Trivia: Lilac Sunday is a day-long celebration held in the Arnold Arboretum in Boston, Massachusetts. It is the only day when visitors are allowed to picnic in the arboretum.

Tanacetum

Common Name: **Feverfew, Tansy, Cow bitter**

Availability: All year round.

Vase Life: Approx 7–14 days.

Flower Notes: Pronounced 'Tan-a-SEE-tum'. A bushy herb of pretty, daisy-like flowers with delicate petals and small, button-like centres. The leaves have a citrus scent when crushed. Medium stem length.

Colour Range: Cheerful yellow, lemon, white.

Tanacetum vulgare

For the Florist:

- Ideal temperature range 2–5°C (36–41°F).
- Remove all leaves in contact with water.
- Change water daily and use flower food.
- Display in cool conditions and keep out of sunlight and direct heat sources.
- Tanacetum can irritate the skin, so always wash hands after using.
- **Stem Type:** Soft.
- **Form:** Transitional.

For the Home:

- Re-cut stems and stand in clean, fresh water which should be changed every day.
- Remove any foliage in contact with water and add flower food.
- Display in a cool spot with good air circulation.
- Use gloves when handling to minimise any possible irritation and wash hands after use.
- Arrange with delicate flowers such as scabious, Nigella or *Alchemilla mollis* for a pretty, summery look.

Tanacetum parthenium 'Single Vegmo'

For Weddings:
As Tanacetum can be an irritant it's probably best to avoid using it in hand-tied designs. However its wild flower meadow look does lend itself to simple vase arrangements where it will complement other dainty flowers. Stems are a little too soft for wiring and for using in floral foam.

For Students:
Family: Asteraceae.
Genus: Tanacetum.
Origin: North Europe and Asia.
Flower Trivia: Its citrus qualities make Tanacetum a good insect repellent, and it has numerous uses in herbal medicine. It should not be consumed 'untreated' however.

Trachelium

Common Name: **Blue throatwort**

Availability: All year round, with different varieties peaking within that period.

Vase Life: Approx 7–10 days.

Flower Notes: Pronounced 'Track-E-lee-um'. A garden perennial with clusters of tiny flowers on slender stems that create a fluffy umbrella-shaped head. Medium stem length.

Colour Range: White, lilac, violet blue, purple, jade green.

For the Florist:

- Ideal temperature range 2–5°C (36–41°F).
- Never leave out of water as Trachelium wilts very quickly.
- Change water every 2–3 days. Flower food is recommended.
- The flowers will continue to open after being conditioned.
- **Form:** Transitional.

For the Home:

- Re-cut stems and stand in clean, fresh water with flower food.
- Stand in a cool spot, and change water every 2–3 days.
- Trachelium lasts well in floral foam and is a very handy filler flower.
- Some people can be allergic to Trachelium, so always wash hands after use.
- The blue and green varieties will complement deep reds and oranges; try them with gladioli or roses.

 Trachelium caeruleum 'Supreme Blue'

For Weddings:
The deeper coloured Trachelium is ideal for autumn and winter weddings, whereas the fluffy white varieties would add a soft texture to spring and summer flowers. Stems are strong enough for arranging in floral foam or for cutting down and adding into tied designs.
Flower Meaning: Neglected beauty.

For Students:
Family: Campanulaceae.
Genus: Trachelium.
Origin: S/W Europe.
Flower Trivia: The name throatwort is related more to the tiny flower's throat-shaped petals than the flower's ability to cure sore throats, of which there is no real proof.

Triteleia

Common Name: **Brodia, Grassnut**

Availability: April–August, peaks June–July.

Vase Life: Approx 14–21 days.

Flower Notes: Pronounced 'Try-TELL-lee-a'. A very pretty summer flowering perennial, not unlike Agapanthus, with funnel-like flowers forming a loose sphere on a slim, leafless stem. Medium stem length.

Colour Range: Lilac, sky blue, deep blue.

For the Florist:

- Ideal temperature range 2–5°C (36–41°F).
- Remove any white parts of the stem as these will not take up water.
- Very sensitive to the effects of ethylene gas and direct heat sources which can cause flower drop.
- Add flower food to the water as this will encourage the buds to open.
- **Stem Type:** Soft.
- **Form:** Line/Transitional.

For the Home:

- Re-cut stems and stand in clean, fresh water.
- Flower food is recommended.
- Change water every 2–3 days and mist occasionally.
- Display at room temperature, out of direct heat and sunlight.
- Contrast the rich colour of Triteleia with the fresh lime of *Alchemilla mollis* or the zesty orange of Calendula.

 Triteleia laxa 'Corrina'

For Weddings:
One of the true blue flowers, Triteleia will add a splash of vivid colour to bridal bouquets and venue designs. Although delicate looking, it lasts well in floral foam and the individual flowers can be wired for boutonnières, corsages and headdresses.

For Students:
Family: Asparagaceae.
Genus: Triteleia.
Origin: North America.
Flower Trivia: Triteleia is sometimes known as triplet lily, as all parts of the flower come in threes. It is synonymous with *Brodiaea laxa*.

Tulipa

Common Name: **Tulip**

Availability: October–June, peaks December–April. Some limited availability out of season.

Vase Life: Approx 5–10 days.

Flower Notes: Available in single, double, lily and parrot forms, tulips never fail to cheer up hearts and homes in the darkest of the winter months. Short stem length.

Colour Range: All colours in single, striped and bicoloured except for blue, green and black.

For the Florist:

- Ideal temperature range 2–5°C (36–41°F).
- Cut away any white ends on the stems as they will not take up water.
- On arrival stand the flowers in water for about an hour before unwrapping.
- Re-cut stems and change water every 1–2 days. Tulips are thirsty flowers, check vase levels daily.
- Tulips will continue to grow after being cut. Wiring the stems can help to control them.
- **Stem Type:** Soft.
- **Form:** Line.

 Tulipa 'Arabella'

For the Home:

- Re-cut stems every 1–2 days and display in clean, fresh water with flower food.
- Tulips are phototropic; to minimise movement, stand them in a spot lit equally from all sides.
- If using in arrangements don't forget that they will continue to grow in floral foam!
- Display in a cool area out of direct heat to maximise vase life.
- Beautiful on their own or add to jugs of Ranunculus and Anemones.

For Weddings:

A popular bridal flower, equally gorgeous when grouped as a tied posy or combined with other delicate spring flowers. Tulips also make great table decorations if arranged in simple containers – but bear in mind that they will continue to move and grow. Use them in buttonholes and corsages with care. **Flower meaning:** Fame.

For Students:

Family: Liliaceae.
Genus: Tulipa.
Origin: S. Europe, N. Africa & Asia.
Flower Trivia: There are various old wives' tales about how to stop tulips from moving around, although in reality there is not much that can be done to stop this from happening – just enjoy them for what they are!

Vanda

Common Name: **Vanda orchid**

Availability: All year round.

Vase Life: Approx 10–21 days.

Flower Notes: A beautiful orchid and one of the very few with a true blue flower (*V. coerulea*). Its pansy-shaped petals have a crystalline texture, making them glisten slightly. Between 5–15 heads per stem. Short to medium stem length.

Colour Range: Violet blue, purple, cerise pink, burgundy, burnt orange.

For the Florist:

- Ideal temperature range 7–15°C (44–59°F).
- Remove packaging and re-cut stems before placing in water.
- Stand in a light spot, but out of direct heat and away from sources of ethylene gas.
- Mist gently to maintain humidity. Limp flowers can be revived by submerging briefly in tepid water.
- **Form:** Line/Round.

For the Home:

- Re-cut stems and stand in clean, fresh water.
- Display at room temperature but away from direct heat which can dry out the flower.
- They prefer a humid atmosphere; mist stems and flowers gently everyday with tepid water.
- Stems of Vanda orchids will trail elegantly from tall vases. Alternatively float single heads in glass bowls with contrasting coloured stones.

 Vanda 'Blue Magic'

For Weddings:

An unusual orchid whose strong colour and form will help to create individual and striking bridal bouquets - this flower is a floral star! Perfect for structured bridal designs although they might be trickier to place in hand-tied posies. Individual heads can be wired or glued for modern corsages and boutonnières.

For Students:

Family: Orchidaceae.

Genus: Vanda.

Origin: S/E Asia and Australia.

Flower Trivia: So popular was the blue orchid when it was first revealed to the world in 1847 that keen collectors rendered it almost extinct. It is now listed as an endangered species.

161

Veronica

Common Name: **Speedwell**

Availability: All year round with different varieties peaking within the year.

Vase Life: Approx 7–10 days.

Flower Notes: A pretty herbaceous plant with slim, delicate spikes covered with tiny flowers that rise from dark green bushy foliage. Medium stem length.

Colour Range: White, pale pink, deep pink, pale purple, violet blue, purple.

For the Florist:

- Ideal temperature range 2–5°C (36–41°F).
- Remove all leaves in contact with water and add flower food.
- Veronica will wilt rapidly if left out of water for any length of time.
- Stand in deep water which should be changed every 2–3 days, re-cutting stems each time.
- **Form:** Line.

For the Home:

- Re-cut stems and stand in clean, fresh, deep water.
- Remove any foliage below the water line.
- Flower food is recommended, change water and re-cut stems every 3–4 days.
- Arrange Veronica with round-headed delicate flowers such as spray roses, Ranunculus or mini sunflowers.

 Veronica 'Anna'

For Weddings:

An excellent choice of flower for adding line and contrast to bridal flowers. Preferably arrange in vases as Veronica will not last long in floral foam. Stems and flowers are also a little too soft for wiring work. Choose pink Veronica for subtle summer colour schemes, and the bolder purple to contrast with rich autumn colours.

Flower meaning: Fidelity.

For Students:

Family: Plantaginaceae.

Genus: Veronica.

Origin: Europe & East Asia.

Flower Trivia: *V. americana* was used as an expectorant by Native Americans, it is supposed to have a taste similar to that of watercress. *V. spicata* is the county flower of Montgomery, Wales.

Viburnum 'Compactum'

Common Name: **European cranberry, Crampbark**

Availability: May–October, peaks June–September.

Vase Life: Approx 10–14 days.

Flower Notes: A compact shrub with clusters of attractive translucent berries and bright green leaves that colour red in the autumn. Tall stem length.

Colour Range: Bright shiny red.

For the Florist:

- Ideal temperature range 2–8°C (36–46°F).
- Viburnum is a thirsty flower so check vase levels regularly.
- Refresh water every 2–3 days, re-cutting stems each time.
- Use shrub flower food if available and remove any unnecessary foliage.
- **Stem Type:** Woody.
- **Form:** Transitional.

For the Home:

- Re-cut stems and place in clean, fresh water.
- Change water every 2–3 days, re-cutting stems each time.
- Removing excess foliage will prolong vase life.
- Use these cheerful berries to add shine and seasonality to vases of Dahlias, Chrysanthemums or sunflowers.

 Viburnum opulus 'Compactum'

For Weddings:

These vibrant red berries are perfect for adding texture and rich colour to late summer/early autumn weddings. Contrast with gold and orange shades in large venue designs with showy large-headed flowers. Suitable for using in floral foam (ensure container is kept topped up) or for wiring into corsages and buttonholes.

For Students:

Family: Adoxaceae.

Genus: Viburnum.

Origin: Northern hemisphere.

Flower Trivia: Despite its common name, the berries are not cranberries and although they can be eaten in small amounts, can have a mildly toxic effect. Probably best avoided!

163

Viburnum 'Roseum'

Common Name: **Guelder rose, Arrow-wood, Snowball tree**

Availability: November–June, peaks January–May.

Vase Life: Approx 7–10 days.

Flower Notes: A popular ornamental deciduous shrub with mop-shaped heads of delicate, tiny flowers on woody stems. Tall stem length.

Colour Range: Creamy green, lime.

For the Florist:

- Ideal temperature range 2–8°C (36–46°F).
- Cut approx 2cm (1″) from the stem with secateurs and place immediately in tepid water.
- Viburnums are thirsty flowers so check vase levels regularly and refresh water every 2–3 days.
- Use shrub flower food if available, and remove any excess foliage.
- Revive wilting flowers by immersing heads briefly in cold water.
- **Stem Type:** Woody.
- **Form:** Transitional.

 Viburnum opulus 'Roseum'

For the Home:

- Re-cut stems with secateurs and place in clean, tepid water.
- Change water every 2–3 days, re-cutting stems each time.
- Removing excess foliage will improve its appearance and prolong its vase life.
- Display out of draughts and direct heat sources.
- Cut into smaller pieces and arrange with Ranunculus or Narcissus for a cheerful spring display.

For Weddings:

Viburnum is a wonderful flower for weddings, particularly in hand-tied posies where it will add a fluffy texture and lightness. Contrast with vivid spring flowers or use it to complement white, cream and lemon. Elegant stems of Viburnum will look impressive in tall table vases, but may wilt a little in floral foam especially on a hot day.

Flower Meaning: Winter.

For Students:

Family: Adoxaceae.

Genus: Viburnum.

Origin: Northern hemisphere.

Flower Trivia: Otzi, the Copper Age Iceman, whose preserved body was discovered in the Alps in 1991, had arrow shafts made from Viburnum in his quiver. The find dates back over 5,000 years.

Zantedeschia

Common Name: **Arum, Calla lily**

Availability: All year round, with main availability between April and October.

Vase Life: Approx 7–14 days.

Flower Notes: Pronounced 'ZANT-a-de-she-a'. A striking herbaceous plant with a single flower at the end of a fleshy thick stem. The 'petal' is actually a spathe, wrapped sheath-like around an upright spadix. Medium/tall stem length.

Colour Range: Pure white, and all shades of pink, yellow, orange, red, green and deepest burgundy.

For the Florist:

- Ideal temperature range 5–10°C (41–50°F).
- Stand in shallow water to prevent the stems from turning slimy.
- Displaying in opaque vases or wrapping the ends with clear tape can help to prevent stems from curling.
- They are thirsty flowers so check vase levels and change water daily.
- **Form: Line.**

For the Home:

- Re-cut stems and place in clean shallow water. Flower food is not necessary.
- Display in a cool spot out of direct heat sources and change water daily.
- The sap can be an irritant so wash hands and tools after handling.
- Zantedeschia don't absorb water from floral foam easily, they must be fully conditioned before use and always keep containers topped up with water.
- Arrange these iconic flowers with sculptural grasses and tropical flowers such as Anthuriums and orchids.

 Zantedeschia 'Captain Prado'

For Weddings:
This elegant flower is a popular choice for both bridal and venue designs. The stems are flexible and can be curved and curled in design work. They are more suitable for arranging in water than in floral foam. Smaller varieties are suitable for wiring work.
Flower Meaning: Ardour.

For Students:
Family: Araceae.
Genus: Zantedeschia.
Origin: Southern Africa.
Flower Trivia: Introduced into Europe in the 1660's, Zantedeschia is thought to have been named after the Italian botanist and physician, Giovanni Zantedeschi.

Zinnia

Common Name: **Zinnia, Youth-and-old-age**

Availability: May–October, peaks July–September.

Vase Life: Approx 6–8 days.

Flower Notes: A popular bedding plant, Zinnia's bold daisy-like flower could well be mistaken for a Dahlia, but its coarse, hairy stem gives it away. Short stem length.

Colour Range: Sunny orange, bright pink.

For the Florist:

- Ideal temperature range 2–5°C (36–41°F).
- Remove any damaged leaves and those in contact with water.
- Change water every other day and add flower food.
- Zinnia is susceptible to mildew, discard any old flowers and display in an area with good air circulation.
- **Form:** Round.

For the Home:

 Zinnia elegans

- Re-cut stems, remove foliage below the water line and stand in clean, fresh water.
- Flower food is recommended, and water should be changed every other day.
- Zinnias should have solid, tight centres which soften as they mature.
- They are thirsty flowers so check vase levels daily.
- Arrange with Calendulas, Tanacetum and lime Chrysanthemum for a bold, vibrant display.

For Weddings:

These pretty summer flowers would be ideal for a bride looking for that natural, 'just picked' look. Although the stems are not robust enough to use in floral foam, they will add a splash of cheerful colour to tied posies and simple, country style vase designs.

Flower meaning: Thoughts of absent friends.

For Students:

Family: Asteraceae

Genus: Zinnia.

Origin: S/W America, Mexico.

Flower Trivia: Popular since the seventeenth century, Zinnias were given their name in honour of the German botanist, Johann Gottfried Zinn, who first described the flower.

A mini floral miscellany

Wedding anniversaries - traditional

1st	Paper	10th	Aluminium or Tin	35th	Coral
2nd	Cotton	11th	Steel	40th	Ruby
3rd	Leather	12th	Silk or Linen	45th	Sapphire
4th	Linen	13th	Lace	50th	Gold
5th	Wood	14th	Ivory	55th	Emerald
6th	Iron	15th	Crystal	60th	Diamond
7th	Copper or Wool	20th	China	65th	Blue Sapphire
8th	Bronze or Pottery	25th	Silver	70th	Platinum
9th	Willow or Copper	30th	Pearl or Ivory		

Rose meanings

Red: I love you, romance, love

Dark red: Unconscious beauty

White: Innocence and purity

Red & white combined: Unity

Red rosebud: Purity and loveliness

White rosebud: Youth, innocence, purity

Pink: Happiness, thankfulness

Dark pink: Gratitude

Yellow: Friendship, gladness

Orange: Fascination, enthusiasm

Peach: Appreciation, sincerity

Lilac: Enchantment

Single rose: Simplicity

Two roses: Engagement

National flowers

Australia: Golden wattle

Canada: Maple leaf

Egypt: Lotus

Finland: Lily of the valley

France: Fleur-de-lis

Germany: Cornflower

India: Blue lotus

Netherlands: Tulip

New Zealand: Kowhai

Russia: Sunflower

Singapore: Vanda orchid

South Africa: King protea

Switzerland: Edelweiss

United States of America: Rose

Did you know…

Rafflesia arnoldii is the world's largest single flower, nearly 3m in diameter.

The smallest known flower is *Wolffia globosa* or Watermeal which measures only 0.3mm across.

The Titan arum (*Amorphophallus titanum*) holds the title of the largest inflorescence in the world, standing at 9' tall.

One of the rarest flowers in the world is the Youtan Poluo. Discovered in China by a nun who found it growing under her washing machine, it is made up of tiny, white sweet-smelling flowers measuring just 1mm across. Legend has it that it blooms once every 3000 years.

UK Saints days:	
1st March	St. David's Day (Wales)
17th March	St. Patrick's Day (Ireland)
23rd April	St. George's Day (England)
30th November	St. Andrew's Day (Scotland)

Floral emblems of the UK:
Daffodil – Wales
Shamrock – Ireland
Red rose – England
Thistle – Scotland

Glossary

Botanical and floristry terms

Annual A plant that completes its entire life cycle in one year.

Bicoloured A flower with two colours.

Bloom A flower or blossom.

Botrytis A fuzzy gray mould which can infect all parts of a plant or flower. It is caused by humid conditions, condensation or lack of air circulation.

Boutonnière A selection of small flowers arranged to create a buttonhole which is traditionally worn by a groom.

Bract A modified leaf, often brightly coloured, found at the base of a flower or cluster of flowers.

Buttonhole A single flower usually backed with foliage, often augmented with buds, berries and decorative wires.

Calyx The outermost layer of a flower which encloses the petals when in bud.

Corsage A selection of usually small and delicate flowers and plant material formed into a design suitable to be worn on a lapel, handbag, wrist or hat.

Deciduous A plant which loses its leaves annually.

Ethylene gas A colourless, odourless gas produced by plants, fruits and vegetables as they ripen. Over exposure to ethylene gas can cause flowers to mature before time and therefore shorten their vase life.

Evergreen A plant which keeps its leaves all year round.

Family A closely related group of flowers and plants sharing common botanical characteristics.

Filler flower A bushy flower which can be used to 'fill' up spaces in arrangements.

Floral foam A manufactured medium which absorbs and holds water and acts as a support for the arrangement of flowers and foliage.

Floret One of the closely clustered small flowers that make up the head of a larger flower.

Floribunda A rose whose blooms are borne in a cluster rather than a single flower.

Focal Flower or plant material which forms the most prominent area in a design.

Flower food Commercially produced powder or liquid designed to improve and extend the vase life of cut flowers and foliage.

Flower form The shape of a flower which determines its position within a design.

Genus A subdivision of flowers or plants within a larger family that closely resemble each other.

Herbaceous A plant whose above ground growth dies down in winter.

Glossary

Hollow stemmed	A stem with either a hollow or soft, pulpy centre.
Latex	A milky, sometimes sticky sap exuded by certain plants.
Line	Flower material with height and structure which leads the eye up, across or diagonally through a design.
Massed	A quantity of the same flower arranged together to create a larger whole.
Node	The point on a stem from which leaves have been, or are attached.
Pedestal design	A large freestanding arrangement suitable for a church or reception venue.
Perennial	A plant that has a life cycle of three seasons or more.
Pipped	The removal of individual florets for wiring into a design such as a corsage.
Phototropic	A plant whose growth is influenced by light, either growing towards, or away from it.
Rhizome	An underground creeping stem which bears leafy shoots.
Semi-woody stem	A stem which contains both soft and woody fibres.
Shower bouquet	A formal tear-drop shaped style of bridal bouquet either wired or arranged in a lightweight holder of floral foam.
Shrub	A plant that has woody stems which are usually branched from the base upwards.
Soft stemmed	A plant with a non-woody stem.
Spadix	A spike-like flower cluster, most commonly seen in the Araceae family. e.g. Anthurium.
Spathe	A large showy bract surrounding a spadix, e. g. Zantedeschia.
Spike	A stem that has flowers attached directly to it.
Structured design	A limited, contemporary style of arrangement with bold, clean cut lines.
Succulent	A plant with fleshy leaves or stems which can retain water.
Textural	Flower and plant material with both visual and physical texture.
Tied posy	Individual stems of flowers and foliage naturally arranged in a spiral before being tied.
Transitional	A branched flower which 'links' one part of a design to another, e.g. spray carnation.
Wiring/wired work	Flowers and foliage individually wired to create a buttonhole, corsage or other floral decoration worn usually for weddings and other formal occasions.
Woody stemmed	A stem composed of woody fibres which doesn't die down over winter.

Index

Common names

Index

Common names

Acknowledgements...

...and thanks

The author would like to gratefully acknowledge the following organizations and sources of reference:

The Royal Horticultural Society Gardeners' Encyclopedia of Plants and Flowers

Flower Council of Holland's Flower and Plant Bank (www.flowercouncil.org.uk)

The Complete Book of Cut Flower Care, Mary Jane Vaughan

The Illustrated Encyclopedia of Cut Flowers, Gilly Love

Foliage for Florists, Society of Floristry

A Field Guide to the Wild Flowers of Britain & Northern Europe, David Sutton

Language of Flowers, Kate Greenaway

RHS Plant Selector (www.rhs.org.uk)

Royal Botanic Gardens Kew (www.kew.org)

Melbourne Market Authority (www.MarketFresh.com.au)

Floral Design Institute Portland Oregon (www.floraldesigninstitute.com)

Flowers & Plants Association (www.flowers.org.uk)

Crocus Garden Nursery (www.crocus.co.uk)

Plantzafrica (www.plantzafrica.com)

Dave's Garden (www.davesgarden.com)

Chrysal (www.chrysal.com)

The Professional Florists' Manual, Lynda Owen

Huge thanks go out to:

Photographer Mark Follon, who good naturedly took charge of numerous boxes of flowers and produced such gorgeous photography.

Holly Peck for providing additional photography (for details see page 2).

Janet Bowyer at Corner House Design & Print for her hard work as always over and above the call of duty. Joy Gill NDSF and Mandy Davis NDSF. Margaret Dunn, Brett Whale, Alison Bradley from Fusion Flowers for her enthusiasm and support, Richard Haslem, Teri Siggins, Lesley Mawditt, Jennifer Bills.

Additional Photo credits

Pages 1 & 114 haru@Shutterstock, 129 Shutterstock & insert 157 Nella@Shutterstock